OPPOSING
VIEWPOINTS®
SERIES

Privacy

Other Books of Related Interest:

Opposing Viewpoints Series
The Information Revolution
National Security
The Patriot Act
The War on Terrorism
Civil Liberties
Students' Rights

Current Controversies Series
America's Battle Against Terrorism
Civil Liberties
Computers and Society
Espionage and Intelligence Gathering
Homeland Security

At Issue Series
Are Privacy Rights Being Violated?
Can DNA Testing Improve America's Legal System?
Gay Marriage
Homeland Security
Racial Profiling
Does the Internet Benefit Society?

"Congress shall make
no law . . . abridging
the freedom of speech,
or of the press."

First Amendment to the U.S. Constitution

The basic foundation of our democracy is the First Amendment guarantee of freedom of expression. The Opposing Viewpoints Series is dedicated to the concept of this basic freedom and the idea that it is more important to practice it than to enshrine it.

OPPOSING VIEWPOINTS® SERIES

Privacy

Jamuna Carroll, Book Editor

GREENHAVEN PRESS
An imprint of Thomson Gale, a part of The Thomson Corporation

THOMSON
GALE

Detroit • New York • San Francisco • New Haven, Conn. • Waterville, Maine • London • Munich

Bonnie Szumski, *Publisher*
Helen Cothran, *Managing Editor*

© 2006 Thomson Gale, a part of The Thomson Corporation.

Thomson and Star Logo are trademarks and Gale and Greenhaven Press are registered trademarks used herein under license.

For more information, contact: Greenhaven Press
27500 Drake Rd.
Farmington Hills, MI 48331-3535
Or you can visit our Internet site at http://www.gale.com

LIBRARY OF CONGRESS CATALOGING-IN-PUBLICATION DATA

Privacy / Jamuna Carroll, book editor.
    p. cm. -- (Opposing viewpoints series)
    Includes bibliographical references and index.
    ISBN 0-7377-3415-9 (hardcover : alk. paper) -- ISBN 0-7377-3416-7 (pbk. : alk. paper)
    1. Privacy, Right of--United States. I. Carroll, Jamuna. II. Series: Opposing viewpoints series (Unnumbered)
    JC596.2.U5P75 2006
    323.44'80973--dc22
                                     2006016376

Printed in the United States of America
10 9 8 7 6 5 4 3 2 1

Contents

Chapter 3: Is Medical Privacy Adequately Protected?

Chapter 4: How Should Privacy Be Protected?

Why Consider Opposing Viewpoints?

> "The only way in which a human being can make some approach to knowing the whole of a subject is by hearing what can be said about it by persons of every variety of opinion and studying all modes in which it can be looked at by every character of mind. No wise man ever acquired his wisdom in any mode but this."
>
> *John Stuart Mill*

In our media-intensive culture it is not difficult to find differing opinions. Thousands of newspapers and magazines and dozens of radio and television talk shows resound with differing points of view. The difficulty lies in deciding which opinion to agree with and which "experts" seem the most credible. The more inundated we become with differing opinions and claims, the more essential it is to hone critical reading and thinking skills to evaluate these ideas. Opposing Viewpoints books address this problem directly by presenting stimulating debates that can be used to enhance and teach these skills. The varied opinions contained in each book examine many different aspects of a single issue. While examining these conveniently edited opposing views, readers can develop critical thinking skills such as the ability to compare and contrast authors' credibility, facts, argumentation styles, use of persuasive techniques, and other stylistic tools. In short, the Opposing Viewpoints Series is an ideal way to attain the higher-level thinking and reading skills so essential in a culture of diverse and contradictory opinions.

In addition to providing a tool for critical thinking, Opposing Viewpoints books challenge readers to question their own strongly held opinions and assumptions. Most people form their opinions on the basis of upbringing, peer pressure, and personal, cultural, or professional bias. By reading carefully balanced opposing views, readers must directly confront new ideas as well as the opinions of those with whom they disagree. This is not to simplistically argue that everyone who reads opposing views will—or should—change his or her opinion. Instead, the series enhances readers' understanding of their own views by encouraging confrontation with opposing ideas. Careful examination of others' views can lead to the readers' understanding of the logical inconsistencies in their own opinions, perspective on why they hold an opinion, and the consideration of the possibility that their opinion requires further evaluation.

Evaluating Other Opinions

To ensure that this type of examination occurs, Opposing Viewpoints books present all types of opinions. Prominent spokespeople on different sides of each issue as well as well-known professionals from many disciplines challenge the reader. An additional goal of the series is to provide a forum for other, less known, or even unpopular viewpoints. The opinion of an ordinary person who has had to make the decision to cut off life support from a terminally ill relative, for example, may be just as valuable and provide just as much insight as a medical ethicist's professional opinion. The editors have two additional purposes in including these less known views. One, the editors encourage readers to respect others' opinions—even when not enhanced by professional credibility. It is only by reading or listening to and objectively evaluating others' ideas that one can determine whether they are worthy of consideration. Two, the inclusion of such viewpoints encourages the important critical thinking skill of objectively evaluating an author's credentials and bias. This evaluation will illuminate an author's reasons for taking a particular stance on an issue and will aid in readers' evaluation of the author's ideas.

It is our hope that these books will give readers a deeper understanding of the issues debated and an appreciation of the complexity of even seemingly simple issues when good and honest people disagree. This awareness is particularly important in a democratic society such as ours in which people enter into public debate to determine the common good. Those with whom one disagrees should not be regarded as enemies but rather as people whose views deserve careful examination and may shed light on one's own.

Thomas Jefferson once said that "difference of opinion leads to inquiry, and inquiry to truth." Jefferson, a broadly educated man, argued that "if a nation expects to be ignorant and free . . . it expects what never was and never will be." As individuals and as a nation, it is imperative that we consider the opinions of others and examine them with skill and discernment. The Opposing Viewpoints Series is intended to help readers achieve this goal.

David L. Bender and Bruno Leone,
Founders

Introduction

> "The [constitutional] framers assumed no general right to privacy because, to state the obvious, criminal and evil acts can be committed in privacy."
>
> —Mark R. Levin,
> author of Men in Black, How the Supreme Court Is Destroying America

> "The right to privacy . . . animates the entire Constitution, Bill of Rights included. The drafters . . . felt no need to state what in their minds was already so obvious."
>
> —Jay Bookman,
> deputy editorial page editor of the Atlanta Journal-Constitution

Although the word privacy is mentioned nowhere in America's founding documents, many citizens—and the courts—have come to see it as an indisputable right. The right to be "left alone" was first mentioned in 1928 by Justice Louis Brandeis in his dissenting opinion in *Olmstead v. United States.* It was not until 1965, though, that the courts specifically referred to privacy as a constitutional right. Since then, the right has evolved through a series of court cases and now, according to the courts, encompasses such contentious actions as abortion.

The right to privacy emerged in *Griswold v. Connecticut* (1965). At the time, roughly thirty states had banned the sale, distribution, and use of birth control. These actions were taken in order to prevent Americans from engaging in recreational or extramarital sex. Professors Robert P. George and David L. Tubbs explain that such laws "sought to promote marital fidelity and stable families by discouraging attempts to avoid the possible consequences of non-marital sexual relations through the use of contraceptives."

The judges in *Griswold* determined that the laws illegally infringed upon married couples' right to marital privacy. The Court maintained that although the Bill of Rights does not mention privacy, its other guarantees establish zones of privacy that must be respected. Justice William Douglas, writing for the Court, elaborated:

> Various guarantees create zones of privacy. The right of association contained in the penumbra of the First Amendment is one. . . . The Third Amendment in its prohibition against the quartering of soldiers "in any house" in time of peace without the consent of the owner is another facet of that privacy. The Fourth Amendment explicitly affirms the "right of the people to be secure in their persons, houses, papers, and effects, against unreasonable searches and seizures." The Fifth Amendment in its Self-Incrimination Clause enables the citizen to create a zone of privacy which government may not force him to surrender to his detriment. The Ninth Amendment provides: "The enumeration in the Constitution, of certain rights, shall not be construed to deny or disparage others retained by the people."

After examining these implicit guarantees of privacy, the *Griswold* Court concluded that married couples should be allowed to make family planning decisions without governmental intrusion.

A chain reaction of privacy cases ensued. Seven years after *Griswold*, the right to use birth control was extended to all adults in *Eisenstadt v. Baird*. The Court reasoned that if married couples retain a right to use contraceptives, then so should single adults, for "the constitutionally protected right of privacy inheres in the individual, not the marital couple." According to the decision, "If the right of privacy means anything, it is the right of the individual, married or single, to be free from unwarranted governmental intrusion into matters so fundamentally affecting a person as the decision whether to bear or beget a child."

*Building upon *Eisenstadt*, the 1973 *Roe v. Wade* decision recognized a general right to privacy. A pregnant single woman (Roe) challenged the constitutionality of legislation that banned abortion unless the mother's life was jeopardized by the pregnancy. She and her supporters felt that women should be permitted to make the personal choice of whether or not to carry out their pregnancy. Siding with Roe, the Court found that "state criminal abortion laws ... violate the Due Process Clause of the Fourteenth Amendment, which protects against state action the right to privacy, including a woman's qualified right to terminate her pregnancy."

Griswold, Eisenstadt, and *Roe* were all cited in a 2003 case affirming the right to sexual privacy, *Lawrence v. Texas*. Texas and several other states, believing that sodomy is an abhorrent sexual act, had legislated against it. A gay male couple caught having sex was convicted under Texas's law, and the case went to court. The *Lawrence* Court found that the statute "furthers no legitimate state interest which can justify its intrusion into the personal and private life of the individual." In consequence, state sodomy laws were overturned. Lambda Legal's Courting Justice Campaign noted, "Gay people, the [*Lawrence*] court held, had the same constitutional right to sexual intimacy as their heterosexual counterparts." Soon after, the Massachusetts Supreme Court cited *Lawrence* in its decision to allow homosexuals to marry.

With each court case upholding the right to privacy, bitter dissention has arisen between people who believe everyone has a right to make personal decisions without governmental interference, and those who maintain that the right to privacy does not extend to actions that may harm individuals or society. In *Opposing Viewpoints: Privacy*, authors continue the debate in the following chapters: Do Counterterrorism Measures Infringe on Privacy Rights? Do Technological Developments

Threaten Privacy? Is Medical Privacy Adequately Protected? How Should Privacy Be Protected? It is clear that Americans continue to disagree about the intentions of the Founding Fathers when they enumerated individuals' rights over two centuries ago.

CHAPTER 1

Do Counterterrorism Measures Infringe on Privacy Rights?

Chapter Preface

After terrorists crashed commercial airplanes into the World Trade Center and the Pentagon on September 11, 2001, investigators discovered that all nineteen of the hijackers had violated immigration laws. As Arizona Senator Jon Kyl notes, "Misuse of immigration law allowed 15 of the 19 September 11 hijackers to enter the United States without completing their [visa] applications or being interviewed." According to the government and many concerned citizens, the attacks underscored the need to better regulate who enters the country and how long they stay. In response, the Department of Homeland Security (DHS) implemented US-VISIT (U.S. Visitor and Immigrant Status Indicator Technology). Designed to track the arrival and departure of nearly all visitors to the United States, the system stores information on each immigrant, including a photograph, all ten fingerprints, and other biometric identifiers. Then, each time a visitor enters or leaves the country, officials verify his or her identity by taking two fingerprints and a photo and comparing these to the information on record. Other data collected under the program include the traveler's nationality, complete name, date of birth, citizenship, passport number and country of issuance, country of residence, complete address while in America, and, where applicable, alien registration number and U.S. visa information. Like many counterterrorism measures passed after September 11, US-VISIT has generated heated controversy.

People for the American Way (PFAW) is one of several rights groups that call US-VISIT a grave invasion of privacy. The organization protests, "A system like US-VISIT poses enormous potential for abuse." The information it collects, PFAW avers, "can be shared with state, local, and foreign law enforcement and used for virtually any purpose. The government has . . . indicated that issuing a final privacy plan is not required by law." The Electronic Privacy Information Center adds that without a complete privacy plan, there are no "specific, enforceable procedures for redress if a visitor is denied entry to the United States as a result of US-VISIT . . . or wants to correct inaccurate, irrelevant, outdated, or incomplete information in the system." Furthermore, civil liberties groups maintain that US-VISIT has never caught a wanted terrorist. Privacy International theorizes, "This is not about terrorism; it is a sophisticated system of immigrant monitoring."

Supporters of US-VISIT counter that it has already identified 372 people wanted for crimes or immigration violations and that it does not intrude upon travelers' privacy. In DHS's contention, "US-VISIT helps to secure our borders, facilitate the entry and exit process, and enhance the integrity of our immigration system while respecting the privacy of our visitors." For one thing, DHS states, the program has a privacy officer who ensures that immigrants' privacy is protected and their concerns addressed. Responding to worries about data confidentiality, the Bureau of Customs and Border Protection asserts, "The new passenger information will be stored in databases maintained by DHS and the Department of State. . . . US-VISIT's state-of-the art software and firewalls will simply make better information more secure."

The tension between privacy advocates and government agencies has heightened since the initiation of the war on terror. The authors in the following chapter examine other contentious counterterrorism measures, presenting conflicting views about when, if ever, Americans' privacy should be restricted in order to enhance national security.

"[I]n the rush to enact the PATRIOT Act, broad new powers were created with insufficient scrutiny given to the wording of most provisions."

Patriot Act Surveillance Powers Violate Privacy

Laurie Thomas Lee

Roving wiretaps allow law enforcement officers to monitor all of the lines of communication used by a suspect under one warrant rather than requiring a separate order for each line. In the viewpoint that follows, Laurie Thomas Lee asserts that by expanding the use of roving wiretaps, the Patriot Act violates constitutional protections of privacy against unreasonable searches. She charges that authorities can, without probable cause, wiretap multiple lines, spy on suspects' Internet usage, and retrieve their voice mail. Alarmingly, someone who uses the same line as a suspect may also be monitored, Lee maintains. This, she cautions, could lead to massive surveillance of average citizens. Lee, an associate professor at the University of Nebraska–Lincoln, specializes in privacy law.

Laurie Thomas Lee, "The USA PATRIOT Act and Telecommunications: Privacy Under Attack," *Rutgers Computer & Technology Law Journal*, vol. 29, Summer 2003, pp. 371–403. Copyright 2003 Rutgers Computer & Technology Law Journal. Reproduced by permission.

As you read, consider the following questions:

1. In Lee's contention, under what circumstances does FISA allow electronic surveillance and physical searches?
2. According to the author, what must law enforcement obtain prior to retrieving unopened voice messages?
3. What Fourth Amendment concern does Lee have with roving wiretaps under FISA?

For many years, wiretaps were authorized with minimal judicial or Congressional oversight. Finally, a landmark Supreme Court ruling limiting surveillance [*Katz v. United States* (1967)] prompted Congress to take a more active role, focusing on privacy issues.

The History of Wiretapping Legislation

In 1968, Congress enacted Title III of the Omnibus Crime Control and Safe Streets Act, commonly known as the "federal wiretapping statute," to create a uniform procedure for domestic electronic surveillance in criminal cases. Title III authorizes law enforcement agents to obtain a warrant to engage in electronic surveillance activities but under limited conditions and only if a judge finds probable cause that the target "is committing, has committed, or is about to commit a particular offense." Congress sought to effectively balance privacy interests against law enforcement needs, and the probable cause requirement was particularly important in meeting Fourth Amendment (search and seizure) scrutiny.

Yet executive authority to engage in foreign intelligence surveillance was not meant to be limited, and abuse continued. To clarify the power of the executive branch in matters of foreign intelligence gathering, Congress enacted the Foreign Intelligence Surveillance Act of 1978 ("FISA"). FISA essentially allows electronic surveillance and physical searches of foreigners and U.S. citizens when there is "probable cause to believe that . . . the target . . . is a foreign power or an agent of a foreign power." Still, standards for obtaining a warrant are much less rigorous than under Title III since the information sought is not for criminal prosecution, but only for intelligence gathering, which does not require a showing of probable cause of a crime. Furthermore, applications for FISA warrants are submitted in secret. Various courts have nonetheless found FISA to be a constitutional balancing of Fourth Amendment rights against national security needs for foreign intelligence gathering.

By the mid-1980s, advances in telecommunications technologies presented new concerns not addressed by Title III. Thus, in 1986, Congress enacted the Electronic Communications Privacy Act ("ECPA") as an amendment to Title III, to update the law's language and to cover such technologies as wireless voice communications, stored electronic communications such as electronic mail, and devices that could record incoming and outgoing telephone numbers dialed. . . .

The PATRIOT Act Is Passed in Haste

When terrorists hijacked planes and struck the World Trade Center towers and the Pentagon on September 11, 2001, the White House and Congress reacted quickly in securing greater executive authority and increased surveillance authority for law enforcement. Widespread fear and public support for combating terrorism and bolstering national security helped spur the effort. Within just six weeks of the attacks, the [George W.] Bush administration successfully ushered in a new law, amending FISA, the ECPA, and Title III, and including a number of provisions that federal law enforcement agencies had sought unsuccessfully for years. On October 26, 2001, the USA PATRIOT Act was signed into law.

Unfortunately, in the rush to enact the PATRIOT Act, broad new powers were created with insufficient scrutiny given to the wording of most provisions. Congress spent very little time studying, debating, or hearing expert testimony on the proposed sections. Normal procedural processes, such as inter-agency review and committee hearings were suspended. As a result, many provisions were not checked for their constitutionality, lack of judicial oversight, and potential for abuse. Furthermore, Congress did not consider the chance that law enforcement might use electronic surveillance to monitor activity unrelated to terrorism.

The following section outlines and examines those provisions pertaining to telecommunications users and providers. Secret electronic surveillance of communications, particularly over the Internet, poses serious concerns as millions of unsuspecting Americans use and rely on information services daily. . . .

At the heart of the Fourth Amendment is the freedom from unwarranted searches and seizures. Yet the PATRIOT Act greatly expands the scope of government authority when it comes to search warrants and subpoenas of telecommunications companies and subscribers. In particular, the PATRIOT Act allows for greater law enforcement access to ISP [Internet Service Provider] and cable company business records and subscriber records, as well as voicemail messages and personal communications property, such as a home computer. . . .

Voicemail

The ability to seize voicemail messages was also made much easier under the PATRIOT Act. Section 209 removes voicemail from Title III purview and treats it as stored data as opposed to stored wire communications. As a result, it essentially allows police to get voicemail messages with only a search warrant instead of the traditional and more difficult to obtain Title III wiretap order.

This new provision puts voicemail on par with e-mail when it comes to government access. Under the ECPA, phone calls were distinct "from non-voice communications such as faxes, pagers, and e-mail," [as writer John L. Guerra explains].

The ECPA controlled law enforcement's ability to gain access to stored electronic communications like e-mail; it did not cover access to stored wire communications like voicemail. It has been argued that since e-mail may include attachments comprised of other types of data, including voice recordings, agents attempting to obtain unopened e-mail from an ISP with a search warrant would be unaware that the suspect's in-box messages contained voice attachments not covered by a search warrant. As a result, the PATRIOT Act provides that stored wire and electronic communications are governed by the same rules. Now, law enforcement agents need to obtain only a search warrant instead of an intercept order to retrieve unopened voice messages stored in voicemail boxes.

By eliminating the burdensome process of obtaining a wiretap order, though, this provision ultimately encourages more government searches. Even case law that required the government to apply for a Title III warrant is now overturned. This provision does, however, sunset in 2005. . . .

Wiretaps Under FISA

Surveillance authority, such as wiretapping, is also greatly expanded by the PATRIOT Act. Considerable leeway is given to law enforcement agents to surreptitiously monitor telephone and Internet communications. The PATRIOT Act specifically extends existing authority to the Internet and expands wiretap authority to nationwide jurisdiction and roving wiretaps. Yet Fourth Amendment privacy protections are lost as law enforcement relies on more lenient FISA standards that do not require a showing of probable cause. In addition, reduced oversight will increase the likelihood of more wiretaps and potential abuse, such as content monitoring and surveillance of large groups of innocent users.

Traditionally, laws governing foreign intelligence gathering have differed from domestic intelligence gathering. Specifically, foreign intelligence gathering is allowed without the

Worrisome Wiretapping

Section 206 [of the Patriot Act] authorizes roving wiretaps: taps specific to no single phone or computer but to every phone or computer the target may use. It doesn't get as much attention as it should. If the government decides to tap a computer at the UCLA library, every communication by every user can theoretically be intercepted. . . .

Along with Section 220, which allows a judge to authorize national wiretaps rather than ones limited to her jurisdiction, this severely undercuts a judge's ability to monitor whether taps are being used appropriately and erodes the . . . Fourth Amendment. . . .

The vast expansion of warrant power is worrisome.

Dahlia Lithwick and Julia Turner, "A Guide to the Patriot Act, Part 3. Should You Be Scared of the Patriot Act?" MSN Slate, September 10, 2003. www.slate.com.

same legal restrictions associated with domestic law enforcement. For example, [the American Civil Liberties Union (ACLU) points out,] "wiretapping conducted under the 1978 Foreign Intelligence Surveillance Act does not contain many of the same checks and balances that govern wiretaps for [domestic] criminal purposes." Historically, if the FBI was investigating a crime, it had to apply for a criminal wiretap under Title III and show probable cause of a crime being committed. But under FISA, the requirements are more lenient, and probable cause of a crime is not needed to justify an intelligence wiretap. Wiretapping conducted under FISA was only authorized, however, "when gathering foreign intelligence information [was] the sole or primary purpose of the surveillance," [asserts the ACLU].

The PATRIOT Act now blurs the line of separation between foreign intelligence surveillance and domestic law enforcement investigations. Section 218 of the Act amends FISA to effectively permit law enforcement agencies to conduct surreptitious wiretaps and searches under the looser standards of FISA. . . .

Unfortunately, the ability to obtain wiretap orders without establishing probable cause of a crime will increase the likelihood that law enforcement will abuse its surveillance powers. For example, police will probably prefer FISA wiretaps because they are easier to obtain. FISA wiretaps are issued in a secret proceeding by a secret FISA court that only looks to see that certifications are present and not "clearly erroneous," [according to Electronic Frontier Foundation]. FISA warrant applications are nearly always granted and unlikely to be challenged. They can last up to 90 days and sometimes longer, as opposed to Title III authority, which lasts only 30 days. Since the orders remain secret, and because FISA does not require notice to be given to a target, "the subject of the order never knows that the government was spying on him" [according to Rachel King and Lamar Smith in *Insight on the News*].

The American Civil Liberties Union . . . has expressed concern, warning "that the secret search and wiretap provisions could lead to an age of Big Brother-like surveillance" [as *SF Chronicle* staff writer Carrie Kirby puts it]. . . .

Roving Wiretaps

The PATRIOT Act also means more "roving wiretaps" can be expected on phone and Internet lines. A roving wiretap allows government agents to "intercept all of a suspect's wire or electronic communications relating to the conduct under investigation, regardless of the suspect's location when communicating" [write Ronald L. Plesser, James J. Halpert, and Emilio W. Cividanes]. Roving wiretaps are not new. In fact, since 1986, the ECPA has allowed law enforcement to follow a suspected criminal purposefully switching from one phone to another in an attempt to thwart a tap, without getting a new warrant. In 1998, Congress created a much looser standard for roving wiretaps by "allowing such surveillance when the target's conduct in changing telephones or facilities has just the effect of thwarting the tap" [maintains the ACLU]. Now, section 206 of the PATRIOT Act expands this authority to FISA court orders, extending the use of roving wiretaps from criminal investigations to terrorist probes and eliminating the probable cause requirement.

Allowing roving wiretaps under FISA creates Fourth Amendment concerns and the potential for abuse. Under the Fourth Amendment, a warrant must specify the place to be searched in order to avoid random searches of innocent bystanders. In the context of electronic surveillance, the Constitution should therefore require law enforcement officers applying for a court order to specify the phone they want to tap. Whether roving wiretaps violate the Fourth Amendment has not been decided by the Supreme Court.

Along the same lines, the ECPA specified that before law enforcement could tap the telephone line of someone besides the suspect, they had to ascertain that the target actually was using the line. The PATRIOT Act, however, does not mandate that law enforcement agents determine whether the target is still "using the phone or other means of electronic communication" [according to King and Smith].

Thus, if the FBI obtains a FISA wiretap order, the FBI could continue its monitoring of all Internet communications at a given site even after the suspect's departure and, thereby invade the privacy of innocent users.

FISA roving wiretaps also pose a greater challenge to privacy because they are authorized secretly (by the Foreign Intelligence Surveillance Court) without a showing of probable cause of a crime. The government need not make any showing to a court that the particular information or communication to be acquired is relevant to a criminal investigation or that foreign intelligence gathering is the primary purpose. Until this provision sunsets in 2005, the result may be [what Kirby calls] a "back door to massive wiretapping."

> "Nothing in ... the entire PATRIOT Act
> ... serves to vitiate or surrender any of
> the rights, privileges and immunities
> guaranteed to American citizens."

Patriot Act Surveillance Powers Protect Americans

Peter M. Thomson

Peter M. Thomson is an assistant U.S. attorney for the Eastern District of Louisiana. In the following viewpoint he argues that the government's need to protect America from terrorist attacks outweighs citizens' Fourth Amendment privacy rights, which he says can be limited in national security investigations. Well-financed and highly trained terrorists, he notes, often thwart authorities' wiretaps by switching phones. To remedy the problem, Thomson claims, the Patriot Act allows federal counterintelligence agents to request roving wiretaps. These allow officials to intercept suspects' communications no matter what phone or Internet line they use. According to Thomson, few such wiretaps are actually issued, and fears that the government will use them to spy on innocent citizens are overblown.

Peter M. Thomson, "White Paper on the USA Patriot Act's 'Roving' Electronic Surveillance Amendment to the Foreign Intelligence Surveillance Act," Federalist Society for Law and Public Policy Studies, April 2004. Reproduced by permission.

As you read, consider the following questions:

1. What are the seven technological advances of the digital age that Thomson says pose difficulties for agents in monitoring suspects' communications?

2. How does the author respond to claims that roving wiretaps could result in charges being brought against non-targeted parties?

3. How does Thomson support his assertion that there are sufficient checks and balances within the FISA framework?

For nearly two decades, commencing shortly after the advent of commercial cellular telephone service in the United States, federal law enforcement officers have had the authority, subject to court approval, to conduct "roving" wiretaps and electronic surveillance on persons suspected of committing federal crimes. A roving wiretap, also called a "multipoint" tap, attaches to a particular subject who utilizes multiple telephones or communications devices, rather than to a particular telephone or device, as in the case of a conventional wiretap. A roving wiretap, therefore, allows law enforcement officers to "follow" a subject and lawfully intercept that person's communications with a single court order when the person's telephone (or other communications device) is subject to change, e.g., because he or she is moving from phone to phone to thwart (or with the effect of thwarting) detection, regardless of the phone used when communicating.

Prior to roving wiretaps, law enforcement agents and federal prosecutors had to invest substantial time and resources in obtaining a separate wiretap order for each additional telephone used by a subject during an investigation. Unfortunately, and quite often, this resulted in a loss of valuable evidence through missed wiretap conversations relating to the criminal activity being monitored.

Enter the PATRIOT Act

In October 2001, in the wake of the catastrophic events of September 11, the President signed into law the USA PA-TRIOT Act, which, in part, expanded law enforcement and foreign intelligence authority in several vital areas of electronic intelligence gathering in an effort to combat terrorism. One specific provision, Section 206 of the Act, modified the Foreign Intelligence Surveillance Act of 1978 (hereinafter "FISA") by extending roving surveillance authority to federal counterintelligence officers engaged in domestic foreign intelligence and counterterrorism investigations.

Thus, prior to Section 206 of the PATRIOT Act, a federal law enforcement officer could employ roving surveillance to gather evidence in a criminal investigation, but a federal counterintelligence officer seeking to collect foreign intelligence information under FISA could not. For example, an FBI agent assigned to the Criminal Investigative Division could employ roving surveillance under Title III [of the Omnibus Crime Control and Safe Streets Act] to gather evidence in a criminal investigation against a suspected drug trafficker or money launderer; however, an FBI agent assigned to the Counterintelligence Division could not employ the same roving surveillance technology under FISA to gather intelligence relating to an al-Qaida [terrorist network] operative present in the United States who was planning to inflict mass casualties with a hijacked airliner.

Unfortunately, the expanded roving authority under FISA pursuant to Section 206 has met with stiff but unmerited opposition by defense attorneys and civil libertarian groups, who fear that Congress may have overstepped its legal limits and infringed upon fundamental American liberties. . . .

Title III and FISA Burden Authorities

[With] the dawn of the digital age, persons began communicating routinely over highly-portable and relatively inexpensive digital cell phones, the Internet, and other advanced personal communications devices such as wireless laptops, two-way paging devices, and "Blackberries." These advances, together with the advent of pre-paid dialing cards and Internet-friendly cell phones, created even more difficulties in attempting to monitor a person who deceptively elects to switch communications devices in a calculated effort to avoid surveillance. Moreover, the [Title III] requirement of demonstrating a target's intent to defeat surveillance [before a roving wiretap may be issued] had created unforeseen and unnecessary impediments to roving wiretap investigations, particularly in the context of the technological boom. Consequently, "intent" to thwart was often difficult to prove in advance of obtaining a roving wiretap order. Thus, for example, prior to obtaining a roving wiretap order law enforcement officers were practically required to overhear a suspect admit (e.g., by means of a conventional wiretap or consensual monitoring) that he intended to use different telephones in an effort to defeat surveillance. . . .

[In 1978] FISA established a classified special court to review electronic intercept applications comprised of seven United States District Court judges (drawn from different circuits) appointed by the Chief Justice of the United States. Applications for FISA intercept orders were required to be approved by the Attorney General, contain specific language identifying the proposed target of the surveillance, and demonstrate probable cause that the target was either a "foreign power" or an "agent" of a foreign power. The application also had to contain: a statement of proposed minimization procedures; a certification that the information sought was foreign intelligence information; a statement addressing the length of time surveillance was required; and, a certification that the information sought could not be reasonably obtained by normal investigative techniques. Most notably, for purposes of this discussion, FISA additionally required that "each of [the locations at which surveillance was to be conducted was] being used or [was] about to be used, by a foreign power or an agent of a foreign power."

The Difficulty of Infiltrating Terrorist Cells

The arrival of September 11, 2001, however, has ushered in a new and foreboding era in the history of terrorism. The "Pandora's Box" of terror has finally been opened and we must now anticipate and defend attacks inside our homeland with weapons of mass destruction that have the potential to dwarf the casualties observed at the World Trade Centers, the Pentagon, and at the rural field in Pennsylvania. Thus, U.S. intelligence agencies are not only faced with detecting and preventing the hijacking of airliners, but also with detecting, intercepting and preventing foreign sponsored terrorists from unleashing biological, chemical and portable nuclear weapons within our borders, all of which constitute a clear and present security threat to this nation. In order swiftly and effectively to meet these daunting challenges, speed and secrecy are of the utmost importance.

Terrorists and hostile intelligence agents are highly trained, well equipped and substantially financed. For example, they employ "fronts" to further their clandestine activities, and they launder funds needed for their operations. They have infiltrated this country, both as individuals and within multiple terrorist "cells." Because of their closed operational structures and strong ties of loyalty, it remains extremely difficult to infiltrate their organizations with undercover assets. Therefore, the ability to eavesdrop unhampered but legally on their secret communications is crucial to the intelligence community's antiterrorism efforts. . . .

Section 206 of the PATRIOT Act therefore seeks to "level the playing field" with well-financed and highly trained terrorists and spies by authorizing federal intelligence agents to seek and obtain court permission to use the same roving surveillance techniques in national security and terrorism investigations that have been used for years by law enforcement agents to investigate criminals. Therefore, Section 206 is a logical and critical extension of a valid, lawful and time-tested criminal investigatory technique to our nation's antiterrorism surveillance efforts.

Criticism of "Roving" Surveillance

Critics and opponents of Section 206 claim that roving FISA surveillance is highly invasive and thereby creates a serious potential for abuse. Some legal scholars have likewise denounced the practice, both in the Title III and FISA context, arguing that it constitutes [in the words of the American Civil Liberties Union (ACLU)] a dangerous "broad expansion of power" that does not incorporate sufficient privacy protections to reduce the risk that innocent third party users might have their right to privacy violated. One criminal defense advocate [Leslie Hagin] went so far as to say that roving authority is "not a power the government needs."

The ACLU, likewise, maintains that roving intercepts are "not limited to the target and will lead to interception of many innocent conversations not involving the target." . . .

The ACLU and other critics [also] maintain that roving surveillance violates the Fourth Amendment's "particularity" requirement. [According to writer Jim McGee,] under the "Fourth Amendment, a warrant must specify the place to be searched in order to avoid random searches of innocent bystanders." "In the context of electronic surveillance," civil libertarians and some scholars [such as Laurie Thomas Lee] argue, "the Constitution should therefore require . . . [federal] officers applying for a court order to specify the phone [or computer or other facility] they want to tap." Otherwise, [SF Chronicle writer Carrie Kirby warns], "the back door to massive wiretapping" might be opened.

Fears About the Patriot Act Are Groundless

For years, federal agents were barred from using tools in counterterrorism work that were readily available to agents pursuing gangsters or drug dealers. . . .

The Patriot Act was designed . . . to plug those gaping holes. The wisdom of doing so is suggested by the fact that [terrorist network] Al Qaeda has not managed to pull off another attack on U.S. soil. The fears some expressed when the law was first enacted—that it would trigger a wave of repression, that domestic dissenters would be silenced—turned out to be groundless.

*Jeff Jacoby, "Overblown Fears About the
Patriot Act," Townhall.com, May 24, 2004. www.townhall.com.*

The Fourth Amendment in a National Security Context

The critics' account is unsatisfactory for a number of reasons. To begin with, the Fourth Amendment's reasonableness requirement does not apply to national security investigations in the same way it applies in criminal cases. The Fourth Amendment protects against "unreasonable searches and seizures." In the law enforcement context, a search is presumptively unreasonable unless conducted pursuant to a warrant. Courts have stated and legal scholars have opined, however, that electronic surveillance conducted for national security purposes by the Executive is likely exempt from the Fourth Amendment—or at a minimum the warrant requirement does not apply—particularly in cases involving foreign powers and their agents.

Notwithstanding such an exemption, however, a different standard of "reasonableness" under the Fourth Amendment is invoked in a national security setting than in a criminal law context. The Supreme Court has recognized [in *United States v. United States Dist. Court* (1972)] that "domestic security surveillance may involve different policy and practical considerations from the surveillance of 'ordinary crime.'" Thus, "[d]ifferent standards may be compatible with the Fourth Amendment if they are reasonable both in relation to the legitimate need of [g]overnment for intelligence information and the protected rights of our citizens." Accordingly, any determination of "reasonableness" within the meaning of the Fourth Amendment in a national security context should balance (a) the duty of the government to protect against national security threats with (b) the dangers to individual privacy interests posed by the relevant electronic surveillance procedure.

Regardless, even if one accepts the proposition that FISA surveillance can lead to Fourth Amendment violations, such as an "incidental" intercept during a roving wiretap at a library, the available remedy is a case by case exclusion of the conversations or other evidence seized by virtue of the roving surveillance order. Therefore, if FBI agents employing FISA surveillance obtain evidence against a non-targeted party that leads to criminal prosecution, the aggrieved defendant retains the right to file a motion to suppress the evidence acquired during the FISA surveillance.

In the context of Title III, a number of federal appellate courts have previously held that roving wiretaps do not violate the particularity requirement. Thus, [as noted in *United States v. Bianco* (1993)] "the safeguards required by congress provide adequate protection to preserve the constitutionality of interceptions of oral conversations when authorized."

The Ninth Circuit spoke directly to the issue (in the context of Title III) in *United States v Petti* [1993] reasoning that the particularity requirement of the "place" to be searched may be substituted with that of the "person" in a roving wiretap setting. Thus, a roving order authorizing a wiretap over all telephones used by a subject does particularly describe the "places" or telephones to be searched, albeit in an unconventional manner, in that only those *specific* telephones (or computers, etc.) used by *that* subject may be tapped. The court noted that the government still has the corresponding obligation to minimize all calls, and that Title III only allows a roving order "if the government establishes to the court's satisfaction that it is impossible to specify the facilities because it is the suspect's purpose to thwart interception by changing them." In concluding that roving wiretaps satisfy the Fourth Amendment's particularity requirement, the Court reasoned that roving surveillance permits no greater invasion of privacy than is necessary to meet "the legitimate needs of law enforcement." . . .

Rights Are Retained

There are a number of additional reasons that serve to refute the claims of Section 206 critics that roving surveillance impermissibly threatens individual liberty and privacy interests. First, there is nothing in Section 206 much less the entire PATRIOT Act, which serves to vitiate or surrender any of the rights, privileges and immunities guaranteed to American citizens under the Constitution. To the contrary, FISA specifically and affirmatively seeks to protect and preserve the inalienable rights guaranteed to American citizens, as well as to aliens lawfully admitted for permanent residence. FISA states that "no United States person may be considered a foreign power or an agent of a foreign power solely upon the basis of activities protected by the first amendment to the Constitution of the United States." Thus, a U.S. citizen (or even an alien admitted for permanent residence) cannot be made the target of an electronic surveillance order solely on the basis of activities secured by the First Amendment. Second, the potential for abuse of power with roving surveillance inheres in any government power. However, the Supreme Court repeatedly has reminded us that the law presumes good faith government conduct. The more relevant focus should be whether sufficient checks and balances exist within the present FISA framework to manage and contain that power. Clearly, sufficient certifications and safeguards do exist—including those of judicial review and Congressional oversight—and the internal security benefits of allowing roving wiretaps outweigh the risks, including the inherent risks of taking no action whatsoever. Third, roving wiretaps are used infrequently. Although the occurrence of roving FISA wiretaps remains classified, an analogy can be made with Title III where roving taps are extraordinarily rare. Within the last year, for example, only several roving Title III wiretap orders (applicable to electronic devices) were granted on the federal level. In fact, between 1999 and 2002, just over 1,000 wiretap orders (federal and state) were granted annually of which, in 2002 for example, only nine (three federal and six by State authority) were roving. . . .

The Benefits Outweigh the Risks

It is critical to our nation's antiterrorism efforts that our intelligence agencies possess the legal capability to intercept all forms of communications utilized by terrorists and hostile intelligence agents. If "one" roving tap leads to the seizure of a large cache of botulism toxin in New York or a portable nuclear bomb in Los Angeles, have the benefits outweighed the risks to personal liberties? Moreover, how does the potential loss of privacy to persons over the Internet, for example, compare to the massacre of several thousand persons, the closure of international airspace, the utter destruction of skyscrapers in New York, an economy in a tailspin, and Americans living in terror and afraid to fly on commercial airliners?

"*The power to search is the power to degrade.*"

Suspicionless Searches of Travelers Invade Privacy

Becky Akers

Safeguards against unwarranted searches no longer exist, laments Becky Akers in the following viewpoint. She explains that the early colonists understood the importance of limiting the government's power to search indiscriminately for evidence of crime. However, after the threat of terrorist hijackings arose in the twentieth century, privacy protections were abandoned in favor of random, suspicionless searches of cars, airports, and traveler's luggage, Akers claims. In her contention this practice subjects many innocent travelers to undeserved privacy invasions and rarely results in the capture of terrorists. Akers writes for numerous sources on topics such as government and civil liberties.

As you read, consider the following questions:

1. According to Akers, how many passengers are searched

Becky Akers, "Undoing the Fourth Amendment," *Freeman: Ideas on Liberty*, vol. 55, October 2005, pp. 20–26. Copyright 2005 Foundation for Economic Education, Incorporated. www.fee.org. All rights reserved. Reproduced by permission.

each week at the nation's airports?

2. What is the purpose of warrants, in the author's opinion?

3. What were the court's determinations in *United States v. Moreno*, as cited by the author?

Carlos Gonzalez, 21, of Weston, Florida, stands spread-eagled while an officer pats him down. When the officer bends to frisk his legs, Carlos lowers his arms without asking permission. The officer snarls, "Hey, we're not even close to being finished. What are you trying to hide?" While a crowd watches, Carlos is ordered to disrobe. He hands over his shoes and belt and empties his pockets as the search continues in mortifying detail.

Warrantless Searches

Is Carlos a convicted criminal entering prison, or is he merely among the 10–15 percent of American citizens whom the Transportation Security Administration (TSA) hauls aside for "additional screening" at the nation's airports? Two million passengers weekly are pawed as if they were felons, though their only crime is catching a flight. And while even suspected murderers are not supposed to be searched without warrants, law-abiding passengers such as Carlos abandon this freedom when they enter an airport as surely as Dante's sinners abandon hope when they enter hell.

The Fourth Amendment is so clearly written that even TSA bureaucrats and Supreme Court justices should be able to comprehend it: "The right of the people to be secure in their persons, houses, papers, and effects, against unreasonable searches and seizures, shall not be violated, and no Warrants shall issue, but upon probable cause, supported by Oath or affirmation, and particularly describing the place to be searched, and the persons or things to be seized." How is it, then, that no warrant is ever produced nor any probable cause cited before passengers are manhandled and bags rummaged?

The answer leads us down a rabbit-hole of court decisions to the Wonderland of postconstitutional America. Ironically, despite its high-tech wands and X-ray machines, its sophistication and jargon, Wonderland's tactics have been copped from a long-dead British king. Nor have the evils that result from those tactics abated over the years.

No "Fishing"

Eighteenth-century British citizens, whether in England or the colonies, were almost alone among the world's peoples in boasting that their homes were their castles, inviolate even from their government. Sir William Pitt described this liberty in November 1783 while addressing the House of Commons: "The poorest man may, in his cottage, bid defiance to all the forces of the Crown. It may be frail, its roof may shake; the wind may blow through it; the storm may enter; the rain may enter; but the King of England may not enter; all his force dares not cross the threshold of the ruined tenement."

Folks lived in peace, their homes and persons sacrosanct. No officer disturbed them unless he had good cause—good enough that he was willing to swear to it—to suspect foul play. Even then, he might not search indiscriminately. He had to specify the place he wanted to search and the object he hoped to find. "Fishing" was not allowed. . . .

The Importance of Warrants

The power to search is the power to degrade. That may explain why government cherishes [the authority to search] as much as free people despise it. Few things short of torture keep men more servile than knowing they may, at their ruler's whim, be prodded, poked, stripped, and humiliated.

However, if we grant that one of government's few legitimate pursuits is to apprehend and try thieves, murderers, and other genuine criminals, we must allow it to search for evidence of the crime. Theoretically, warrants balance the state's need to search with the citizen's right to privacy. They severely limit governmental power over the suspected individual—who, at this point has not been convicted of any crime—by specifying the particulars of what can be searched as well as the items sought. Obviously, the more items the state declares illegal, the more essential to freedom these limitations become: allowing government to search indiscriminately means it will find and punish the possessors of drugs, guns, or any of the million and one other things it bans.

[In 1761 lawyer James] Otis listed the malignancies that multiply when specific warrants are abandoned in favor of general searches, malignancies threatening us today. First were the numbers of people who could procure a writ. No longer were a few, specially deputized officers permitted to search. Rather, "Every one with this writ may be a tyrant; if this commission be legal, a tyrant in a legal manner, also, may control, imprison, or murder any one within the realm."

Airport Screeners Have Too Much Power

Otis could have been speaking of the TSA. The agency employs about 45,000 screeners, some with criminal backgrounds. It also boasts about how quickly it hired these people; no wonder the screeners weren't screened. Nevertheless, they wield enormous power over the passengers who fall into their hands. One bragged to magician/comedian Penn Jillette, "Once you cross that line, I can do whatever I want." Another confiscated a passenger's cigarette lighter after exclaiming that he'd always wanted one like it. The passenger reported him to a supervisor but received no satisfaction, so he threatened to contact TSA authorities. The supervisor replied, "Go ahead and complain, there is *nothing you can do to us.*"

"In the next place," Otis observed, general searches are "perpetual; there is no return. A man is accountable to no person for his doings. Every man may reign secure in his petty tyranny, and spread terror and desolation around him."

Random Searches Are Not Justified by the Threat of Terrorism

The New York City Police Department has adopted and is enforcing a criminal, law-enforcement policy and practice of searching the possessions of those seeking to enter the New York City subway system without any suspicion of wrongdoing whatsoever. Since the subway search policy was put into effect on July 21, 2005, police officers have searched the purses, handbags, briefcases, and backpacks of thousands and perhaps tens of thousands of people, all without suspicion of wrongdoing. . . .

The plaintiffs [in this case] are law-abiding New Yorkers who ride the New York City subway system daily and who routinely carry into the system bags containing personal items and private materials. All of the plaintiffs are subject to potential search under the NYPD search policy, and some already have been searched by police officers. All of the plaintiffs object to the police searching their personal possessions as a condition of entering the subway.

The constitutional right of people not suspected of any wrongdoing to be free from police searches is one of the most fundamental protections of our free society. While concerns about terrorism of course justify—indeed, require—aggressive police tactics, those concerns cannot justify the Police Department's unprecedented policy of subjecting millions of innocent people to suspicionless searches in a way that is virtually certain not to identify any person seeking to engage in terrorist activity.

New York Civil Liberties Union, "Preliminary Statement in
Brendan MacWade et al. v. Raymond Kelly and
the City of New York," 2005.

When an officer is not looking for a specific item in a specific place, his search never ends. . . .

The TSA searches all passengers and their baggage. Without any grounds, without even a specific suspicion of a specific passenger, screeners search the flying population at large. The fact that passengers are going about their business peacefully, that they have done nothing to warrant suspicion, much less a search, means nothing. Furthermore, no judge interposes between the citizen and the state. The searches are both sanctioned and conducted by the executive branch of the federal government. . . .

The Feds [decided] to "protect" aviation after a couple of hijackings in the 1960s and early '70s (dignified as an "observable national and international hijacking crisis" in one decision). Then, in 1974, government made the scary leap from apprehending criminals after they had committed a crime to preventing them from committing it in the first place. The courts declared (in *United States v. Moreno*) that "the hijacker must be discovered when he is least dangerous to others and when he least expects confrontation with the police. . . . In practical terms, this means while he is still on the ground and before he has taken any overt action." In practical terms, it also meant that any passenger could be a hijacker. All passengers and their luggage, therefore, must be searched.

The Government Wins

The Fourth Amendment might have reared its pesky head here had it not already sustained some serious wounds. In *Silverman v. United States* (1961) the Supreme Court announced that the Founders intended the Fourth to secure a man's right to "retreat into his own home and there be free from unreasonable governmental intrusion." However true that statement was, subsequent decisions emphasized that *only* in his home might a man be free from governmental intrusion; he abandoned such an expectation once he stepped outside. From this sprang much slicing and dicing of freedom, including the bizarre notion that neither automobiles nor public areas such as airports afford the same level of privacy and freedom from the government as homes, so cops may search the former with far more impunity than they do the latter. . . .

Neither the innocence of the vast majority of passengers nor the effectiveness of the search matter. "Nor would we think . . . that the validity of the Government's airport screening program necessarily turns on whether significant numbers of putative air pirates are actually discovered by the searches. . . . By far the overwhelming majority of those persons who have been searched . . . have proved entirely innocent . . ." (*Nat'l Treasury Employees Union v. Von Raab*). The government wins either way, whether it discovers hijackers or not.

"*Most Americans were perfectly willing to go along with law enforcement officials who suggested that bags should be searched.*"

Suspicionless Searches of Travelers Protect Civil Liberties

Ben Shapiro

After terrorist bombings of public transit systems in London killed more than fifty people in 2005, U.S. officials began to randomly search people on subways in certain cities. Ben Shapiro maintains in the following viewpoint that once searches and other measures have secured the country against terrorism, Americans' civil liberties can and will be fully restored. Until then, random searches of travelers are necessary, he insists. Although he concedes that such searches are a governmental intrusion, he emphasizes that they are among the least invasive counterterrorism measures. Besides, Shapiro points out, Americans' safety is well worth the hassle of having city workers search their bags. Conservative Ben Shapiro is the youngest nationally syndicated columnist in the United States.

Ben Shapiro, "This Is a War, Blockhead," Townhall.com, July 27, 2005. Copyright © 2005 Creators Syndicate, Inc. By permission Ben Shapiro and Creators Syndicate, Inc.

As you read, consider the following questions:

1. In Shapiro's contention, the July 22, 2005, shootings served as a reminder of what?
2. What three examples does the author give of sacrifices that have been made in wartime?
3. What is one option for people who do not want to be searched, as explained by Raymond Kelly?

On July 7 [2005], Muslim terrorists bombed the London Underground trains, as well as a bus in Tavistock Square. Over 50 people were killed, and over 700 were injured.

On July 21, Muslim terrorists attempted to bomb both a bus and the London Underground once again. The following day, British police, suspecting that an overcoat-wearing man could possibly be attempting a terrorist act, chased him into the subway and shot him five times, killing him.

Most Americans reacted to the July 7 bombings with horror. The bombings renewed our sense of vulnerability. The July 21 bombings reiterated the message that Muslim terrorists still wish us all dead; the July 22 shootings reminded us that in a state of war, all of us must retain the utmost respect for law enforcement.

So most Americans were perfectly willing to go along with law enforcement officials who suggested that bags should be searched at subway stations in Washington, D.C., and New York. Yes, we'd prefer that police target those of Muslim religious persuasion for searches: After all, bombers tend not to be middle-aged white women from Kansas or elderly Asian men. Random searches are worse than useless, because they provide the illusion of security. But that doesn't mean we should resist police enforcement or lobby against further enforcement.

Some Civil Liberties Must Be Sacrificed

Most of us realize that during wartime, sacrifices must be made. During the Civil War, President Lincoln famously suspended writs of habeas corpus. During World War I, Congress passed the Espionage Act, prescribing harsh penalties for anyone revealing defense information or preventing the recruitment of troops. During World War II, thousands of Japanese were interned because President Franklin Roosevelt had information suggesting that some American Japanese were aiding the enemy.

Surely, having our bags checked does not even begin to approach such heavy-handed and horrific measures. As New York Police Department Commissioner Raymond Kelly explained, those who do not want their bags to be checked can simply opt not to take the subway. Communal safety supersedes any supposed individual "right" to transportation here. Effective law enforcement should supersede individual "rights" to transportation when hundreds, potentially thousands, of human lives are at stake.

But taking such a stand requires common sense and the knowledge that we are in the midst of the great battle of our time. Some Americans lack both common sense and knowledge. Such people maintain all this war talk is nonsense—we are simply being misled by a government that seeks to remove our civil liberties in order to establish a fascistic regime. One such person, Tony Lu, a New York "immigrant rights activist," decided that resisting the NYPD was far more important than allowing police to fight terrorism. And so the day of the second London bombing attempt, Lu designed a T-shirt reading "I do not consent to being searched."

This is obnoxious and wrongheaded. Yes, governmental intrusion can be scary. Yes, we would all prefer to ride the subway without the hassle of having security employees rifling through our bags. But most of us would also prefer not to be

Stantis. © 2003 *USA Today*. Copley News Service. Reproduced by permission.

blown up, and if that entails having some uniformed city worker check my backpack, so be it.

Denial

Unfortunately, Lu is not alone in his refusal to acknowledge the reality that we are at war. The American Civil Liberties Union [ACLU] focuses far more on preventing effective law enforcement than on protecting American lives. Its incessant complaints about the treatment of Guantanamo Bay[1] detainees has undermined the moral authority of the American military, despite the fact that treatment has been more than adequate under the circumstances. Its obsession with "exposing" as many Abu Ghraib images[2] as possible is designed as a direct attack on American soldiers abroad. It is no wonder that American soldiers at Guantanamo hotly castigated ACLU

1. The U.S. Naval base at Guantanamo Bay, Cuba, holds prisoners suspected of fighting against the United States in the war on terror.

2. In 2004 photos of U.S. soldiers allegedly torturing Iraqi prisoners at Abu Ghraib Prison in Iraq were released.

allies [Senators] Teddy Kennedy and Daniel Akaka for the obscene Democratic rhetoric regarding prisoner treatment.

But civil libertarian absolutists will continue to assault America's safety in favor of American "liberties." Myopic civil libertarians ignore the simple fact that effective law enforcement is the best way to promote civil liberties. If we live in a safe, secure country—if we rid ourselves of threats domestic and foreign—there is no need for harsh safety precautions. Habeas corpus was restored after the Civil War. Free speech protections were strengthened in the aftermath of World War I. Japanese internment ended after World War II. Temporary safety measures remain in force only as long as safety is threatened. If civil libertarians undermine such measures, they threaten our safety—and temporary measures become more and more permanent. The only way to fully restore civil liberties is to defeat our enemies.

"When we can verify identity, we're one step closer to preventing fraud, protecting privacy, and saving lives."

A National Identity Card Would Preserve Privacy

Betty Serian

Numerous problems arise from the lack of a uniform driver's license, contends Betty Serian in the following viewpoint. Because there are many different forms of IDs and practices for issuing IDs in different states, terrorists and identity thieves have many points at which to exploit the system, Serian maintains. She notes that hijackers have boarded planes using IDs obtained with fraudulent documents. In Serian's opinion, these vulnerabilities can be addressed, and identities protected, by creating a standard ID card across the states and training workers to recognize fake documents. Serian delivered this speech at a U.S. Senate hearing on April 16, 2002. She is on the board of directors for the American Association of Motor Vehicle Administrators, a trade organization of state officials who enforce motor vehicle laws.

Betty Serian, testimony for "A License to Break the Law? Protecting the Integrity of Driver's Licenses," hearing of the Senate Committee on Governmental Affairs, Subcommittee on Oversight of Government Management, Restructuring, and the District of Columbia, April 16, 2002.

As you read, consider the following questions:

1. What were the results of the Public Opinions Strategies poll, as cited by the author?
2. According to Serian, which fraudulent breeder documents are commonly used to obtain IDs?
3. What are Serian's five recommendations to Congress?

The driver's license has become much more than a license to drive. Over the last 40 years, the use of the driver's license changed due to the demand for identification put on the public by the private sector.

Now, allow me to tell you three stories about a few Americans.

Larry and Rita Beller and Edward and Alice Ramaeker, four retirees, spent their golden years traveling across the country. Earlier this year [2002], they were killed on a New Mexico highway by a repeat DWI offender. The driver, holding eight prior convictions from different states, was under the influence of alcohol and plowed head on into the retirees' car.

Emeke Moneme, an Ohio resident, had his wallet stolen from a local gym. Within weeks, Emeke discovered an identity thief had opened 13 fraudulent accounts in his name, totaling $30,000 in bad credit debt. It took him months to clear his name and straighten out his life.

Sarah Clark, a schoolteacher and newly engaged, was killed after her flight was overtaken by terrorists and crashed into the Pentagon. Terrorists boarded the ill-fated flight using fraudulently obtained driver's licenses.

- Sarah Clark shared her sad fate with more than 3,000 other Americans on [September 11, 2001].

- Larry and Rita Beller, and Edward and Alice Ramaeker, share the list of DWI fatalities with more than 16,000

Americans each year.

- And, Emeke Moneme shares victimization by identity theft with hundreds of thousands of Americans. Stealing someone's identity information, such as credit cards or Social Security Numbers, to take money or commit fraud is one of the fastest-growing crimes in the U.S. According to the Federal Trade Commission, 42% of the 204,000 complaints filed [in 2001] involved identity theft—resulting in billions of dollars of loss.

A Lack of Uniformity

A common thread to these tragedies? The driver's license. In fact, the driver's license has become the most requested form of ID in the U.S. and Canada. For example, financial institutions require it to open an account, retail outlets ask for it when you want to pay by check, and the airlines demand it before you board a plane. In a recent (April 2002) poll conducted by Public Opinion Strategies, 83 percent of the American public noted that they used their driver's license for purposes other than driving.

The U.S. has more than 200 different, valid forms of driver's licenses and ID cards in circulation. In addition, each of the 50 states and D.C. have different practices for issuing licenses. Although the current system allows for reciprocity among the states, *it lacks uniformity*. Individuals looking to undermine the system, whether it is a terrorist, a drunk driver or an identity thief, shop around for licenses in those states that have become the weakest link.

In addition, the lack of standard security features on a driver's license allows individuals to exploit the system. While all states use a variety of security techniques, it is difficult for law enforcement and for those issuing a new license to verify the validity of a license from another state—not to mention the identity of the person holding the license. This situation is worsened by the availability of counterfeit driver's licenses and fraudulent breeder documents, such as a birth certificate or Social Security card, over the Internet and on the underground market.

Improving Uniformity for the Driver's License/ID Card

We at AAMVA [American Association of Motor Vehicle Administrators] commend you, Senator [Dick] Durbin, for your focus on the need for a comprehensive reform of the driver's licensing process and identification security. In the days following September 11, Americans quickly learned how easily terrorists obtained a driver's license. All of the terrorists either legally or illegally obtained valid or bogus licenses and ID cards. What is saddening, is that it took this catastrophic event to heighten America's awareness to the importance of ensuring the security of ID credentials—like the DMV [Department of Motor Vehicles]–issued driver's license.

In October 2001, the AAMVA Executive Committee developed and passed a resolution establishing the Special Task Force on Identification Security. The Task Force was organized into five working groups focusing on technology, new issuance/initial identification, residency issues, document security/standards and communications/advocacy. The working groups produced reports that addressed the current situation and identified gaps, key issues, barriers, conclusions and results. The Task Force concluded that there were a number of common issues needing to be addressed: administrative processing, verification/information exchange, the need for a unique identifier, the format of the driver's license/ID card, fraud prevention and detection, residency, and enforcement and control of standards.

In January 2002, the Task Force recommended eight broad strategies, [including:]

  1. Improve and standardize initial driver's license and ID processes.

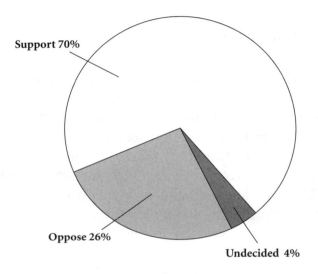

Americans' Opinions on Mandatory National ID Cards

Support 70%

Oppose 26%

Undecided 4%

SOURCE: Compiled by Jamuna Carroll using statistics from the University of Michigan Institute for Social Research, 2002.

2. Standardize the definition of residency in all jurisdictions.

3. Establish uniform procedures for serving noncitizens.

4. Implement processes to produce a uniform, secure, and interoperable driver's license/ID card to uniquely identify an individual.

5. Establish methods for the prevention and detection of fraud and for auditing of the driver's license/ID processes. . . .

AAMVA has identified and targeted the areas that need improvement to reform the driver's license/identification process to achieve the recommendations from the Task Force. . . .

Fraud Prevention Programs

The use of fraudulent documents has caused enormous economic losses in both the U.S. and Canada. In the early 1990s, in conjunction with NHTSA [National Highway Traffic Safety Administration] and the Florida Division of Motor Vehicles, AAMVA, under contract with West Virginia University, developed and implemented a training program including model training materials for the Fraudulent Identification Prevention Program (FIPP). A revision of FIPP training materials was then completed in April 1996. Most recently, the use of fraudulent documents has become a national security issue for both countries as well as foreign countries. The use of fraudulently obtained identification is also directly related to losses in human life on our highways. The use of fraudulent documents to obtain driver's licenses/identification cards has grown exponentially in recent years. Services for obtaining fraudulent documents are easily available through the Internet and other means. In addition, fraudulent breeder documents (Passports, Visas, Social Security Cards, birth certificates, INS [Immigration and Naturalization Service] Documents, driver's licenses or Identification Cards), which are commonly forged, altered or counterfeited, are commonly used to obtain valid driver licenses.

For years AAMVA has provided Fraudulent Document Recognition Train-the-Trainer courses throughout the U.S. and Canada. AAMVA has educated hundreds of fraud recognition trainers for state and provincial motor vehicle agencies. AAMVA has recognized the need to revise existing training materials as well as the need to establish a more comprehensive national model-training program for state and provincial driver licensing personnel and law enforcement officials for the recognition of fraudulent documents. We are updating this course in cooperation with various federal agencies. However, interim training will continue during this revision. AAMVA is creating a "best practices" document that will provide an overview of how state and provincial motor vehicle and law enforcement agencies deal with these issues.

A Standardized, More Secure Driver's License/ID

AAMVA is involved in creating a driver's license document standard, both nationally and internationally. Work began in 1996. National and international standards ensure that documents are interoperable among the issuing jurisdictions—the bar code on an Iowa license may be read by a trooper in New York and vice versa. On a national level, AAMVA has developed and published the AAMVA Driver's License/ID Card Standard that is being used by some states for creating a driver's license and ID card. AAMVA is in the process of further improving this standard and working with more states to ensure that they adhere to its provisions when they create a new document. We continue to work toward further harmonization among the states in using the standard.[1] . . .

The American public wants a more secure license. Seventy-seven percent (77%) of the American public support Congress passing legislation to modify the driver's licensing process and identification security. And, we need Congress to help in five areas:

1. Support minimum compliance standards and requirements that each state must adopt when issuing a license.
2. Help us identify fraudulent documents.
3. Support an interstate network for confirming a person's driving history.
4. Impose stiffer penalties on those committing fraudulent acts.
5. And, provide funding to make this happen. Funding so states can help ensure a safer America.

1. In May 2005, Congress passed the Real ID Act, which encourages states to standardize their procedures and requirements for issuing drivers' licenses.

Our goal is one driver, one license and one driving history. The American people expect Congress to reduce the number of people being victimized by dangerous drivers and identity theft. Most importantly, the American people expect you to do what you can to save lives—to prevent deaths of people like Larry and Rita Beller, Edward and Alice Ramaeker, Sarah Clark and thousands of other Americans. When we can verify identity, we're one step closer to preventing fraud, protecting privacy, and saving lives.

> *"National ID cards would become our passports to commercial transactions, to travel, to employment, and even to our most personal interactions."*

A National Identity Card Would Compromise Privacy

Charles Levendosky

According to Charles Levendosky in the following viewpoint, a national ID card system meant to keep terrorists from obtaining IDs fraudulently would allow the government to track Americans' every move. The uniform ID, he claims, would contain private details, including Social Security numbers, biometric identifiers, and medical information. This highly sensitive data would be shared with government agencies, insurance companies, and commercial organizations, Levendosky predicts. Errors in the database, he warns, would be difficult to correct and could keep a person from driving or from obtaining medical insurance or a job. Furthermore, he argues, the system would not prevent terrorists from using fake documents to get a national ID. Levendosky, an expert on the Bill of Rights, was the editorial page editor of the Casper (Wyoming) Star-Tribune.

Charles Levendosky, "National ID Cards Strangle Liberty, Banish Privacy," *Liberal Opinion Week*, vol. 13, March 11, 2002, p. 22. Reproduced by permission of the literary estate of Charles Levendosky.

As you read, consider the following questions:

1. What does Levendosky predict will happen to people who don't carry their ID card?

2. In the author's opinion, what entities would be able to access the information on citizens' ID cards?

3. How would a national ID create a false sense of security, as cited by Levendosky?

Just what this country needs—national identity cards, like a system of internal passports. Americans will become foreigners in their own land: "May I see your papers, please?" Each time a citizen applies for a job, a car loan, or health insurance; every time we rent a car or purchase an airline ticket, "Let me see your federal ID, please."

Under a proposal by the American Association of Motor Vehicle Administrators (AAMVA), a national data system will record our every move, tracking us across the country.[1] AAMVA—a trade organization of state officials who administer and enforce motor vehicle laws—wants the federal government to authorize and fund a proposal to standardize state drivers' licenses and link state databases.

The proposal will cost taxpayers at least $4 billion, according to the Social Security Administration. Other estimates put the cost at $9 billion.

An Ill-Conceived Policy

No one is forced to obtain a driver's license, nevertheless 228 million Americans currently have them, and in many commercial transactions a driver's license is a preferred identification. So the argument that the AAMVA proposal doesn't create a national ID system is a distinction without substance. It

---

1. Although the proposal failed to gain Congressional support, another bill passed in May 2005 called the Real ID Act. It standardizes regulations for issuing driver's licenses, and some people believe it will lead to the creation of a national ID card.

is likely that if the identity system went into effect, the failure to carry an ID card would become a reason for detention or a search.

A national identity system is one more ill-conceived public policy that has been precipitated by the terrorist attacks of Sept. 11 [2001]. It won't make us any safer, but it will surely strangle our sense of freedom.

AAMVA would authorize the sharing of the information on citizens' identity cards with the Social Security Administration, Immigration and Naturalization Service, the Federal Bureau of Investigation, other agencies concerned with national security, state agencies, insurance companies and similar commercial organizations.

Highly Sensitive Information

The information the AAMVA would like to have on these identity cards goes far beyond name, address, Social Security number, birth date, weight, height, hair and eye color. The proposal would include medical and disability information as well as encoded biometric identifiers like retinal scans and fingerprints.

Much of that personal information will be easy to access with the proper computer whenever the ID is used in health clubs, banks or grocery stores.

By law, the Social Security card was to have had limited use—to identify the taxpayer as a legitimate recipient of Social Security. Now our Social Security numbers appear on drivers' licenses and health insurance cards and are used as passwords for credit cards. Obviously, national ID cards would become our passports to commercial transactions, to travel, to employment, and even to our most personal interactions.

What becomes of our personal privacy, our right to be left alone, our right to control information about ourselves? Can liberty exist in such a scheme—squeezed between a gigantic

A British Government Agency Speaks Out Against National ID Cards

We are not fundamentally opposed to the idea of ID Cards, but we do have a series of concerns in relation to the legislation and the possible impact the current recommendations could have on personal privacy. The legislation is not just about ID cards—an extensive national identity register/ database and a national identity registration number are also planned. These raise substantial data protection concerns. . . .

Putting all your eggs in one basket may be convenient but this can be risky. If the system doesn't work or isn't administered properly you could find yourself not being able to access a significant range of services if they depend on one, just one, identity document and one set of information. Safeguards must be put in place to ensure individuals' personal information is protected and safe, the system is administered properly and that individuals are not disadvantaged if things go wrong. . . .

A concern to many individuals is that this large central database will note each time the individual's file on the Register is accessed, providing the government and others with access to a comprehensive picture of how we live our lives. The database therefore risks altering the whole relationship between us as individuals and those who govern us.

Information Commissioner, "ID Cards Q&As."
www.ico.gov.uk.

federal bureaucracy and a national computer database stocked with personal information about each one of us?

Anyone who has tried to correct an error in a credit report understands the nightmare that a national ID system would produce. A few wrong key strokes entered into a person's identity record could keep that person from being able to obtain medical insurance, a job, or even a bank loan. The person would be legally prohibited from driving. And because of the massiveness of the bureaucracy involved, it could take years to set the record straight.

Facilitating Fraud

A national ID system won't make us any safer from terrorists or criminals. The basic documents which are used to apply for this identity card would be birth certificates and Social Security cards. These documents are easily forged.

And according to a [2001] story in the *Orange County Register*, 127 California Department of Motor Vehicle [DMV] employees were disciplined over the [previous] five years for facilitating ID fraud.

A national identity card cannot be effective as a useful deterrent against terrorism, as long as the documents needed to obtain that ID card can be forged or a false ID card can be acquired from DMV officials.

A report issued [in 2002] by the Electronic Privacy Information Center points out that a "national ID would create a false sense of security because it would enable individuals with an ID—who may in fact pose security threats—to avoid heightened security measures."

A national identity card system would undoubtedly beget and propagate a surveillance society of sweeping proportions. Where could freedom hide then? Where would privacy conceal itself so that as human beings we can maintain a sense of autonomy, a sense of breathing space and a place to be ourselves?

Periodical Bibliography

Electronic Frontier Foundation — "Let the Sun Set on PATRIOT." www.eff.org.

Amitai Etzioni — "You'll Love Those National ID Cards," *Christian Science Monitor*, January 14, 2002.

Amy Goodman — "Subway Shakedowns: Necessary Security or Unconstitutional Violation?" *Democracy Now!* July 28, 2005. www.democracynow.org.

Rich Haglund — "What Happens to the Fourth Amendment When the USA Patriot Act Enters Wireless Hot Spots?" *Journal of Internet Law*, July 2005.

Nicholas D. Kristof — "May I See Your ID?" *New York Times*, March 17, 2004.

Dahlia Lithwick and Julia Turner — "A Guide to the Patriot Act, Part 3. Should You Be Scared of the Patriot Act?" MSN Slate, September 10, 2003. www.slate.com.

Jeffrey Page — "It's a New World, So Searches Are No Big Deal," *Record (Bergen County, NJ)*, August 5, 2005.

Bruce Schneier — "National Insecurity Cards," *Crypto-Gram Newsletter*, April 15, 2004. www.schneier.com.

Gene Stephens — "Can We Be Safe and Free? The Dilemma Terrorism Creates," *USA Today (Magazine)*, January 2003.

U.S. Department of Justice — "USA PATRIOT Act Overview." www.lifeandliberty.gov.

CHAPTER 2

Do Technological Developments Threaten Privacy?

Chapter Preface

With new technological developments come additional implications for personal privacy. One emerging technology at the center of heated debate is a tracking system called GPS (Global Positioning System). It utilizes twenty-four satellites orbiting the earth that continuously emit signals. When the signals are picked up by receivers on the ground, they are converted into an exact longitude, latitude, and altitude. Lost hikers or drivers, for example, can use a GPS device to determine their precise location. But in addition to noting where a person is, GPS can reveal where a person *has been*. This application has been used by the military, law enforcement, employers, and others who need to monitor people's movements. Like many technologies, GPS offers myriad benefits while at the same time creating potential threats to personal privacy.

An especially contentious application of GPS is when police officers affix GPS trackers to suspects' vehicles without a warrant. Several conflicting lower court decisions have been handed down on the matter. Some people claim that the warrantless use of GPS is an unconstitutional invasion of privacy, since the Fourth Amendment requires officers to obtain a court order before conducting a search of a suspect. Many citizens also fear that this use of GPS by authorities could lead to widespread, unregulated surveillance. To their relief, the Washington Supreme Court declared in 2003 that police must receive a warrant before attaching a tracker to a suspect's vehicle. Justice Barbara Madsen observed that GPS can reveal intimate details about a person. According to Madsen,

> The device can provide a detailed record of travel to doctor's offices; banks; gambling casinos; tanning salons; places of worship; political party meetings; bars; grocery stores; exercise gyms; places where children are dropped off for school, play, or day care; the upper-scale restaurant and the fast

food restaurant; the strip club; the opera; the baseball game; the 'wrong' side of town; the family planning clinic; the labor rally. In this age, vehicles are used to take people to a vast number of places that can reveal preferences, alignments, associations, personal ails and foibles.

Many judges have agreed that the use of GPS to trace a suspect's movements amounts to a search and thus requires a warrant.

Other justices and members of law enforcement, however, contest this notion. They do not consider GPS tracking as any more intrusive than an officer tailing a suspect in a car (a type of surveillance that does not require a court order). According to the 1967 *Katz v. United States* decision, an incident is considered a search only if it occurs where a person has a reasonable expectation of privacy. As assistant U.S. attorney David Grable points out, "Your movements on a highway aren't private." Echoing this sentiment, New York federal judge David Hurd ruled in a 2005 case that a suspect "had no expectation of privacy in the whereabouts of his vehicle on a public roadway." He continued, "Thus there was no search or seizure and no Fourth Amendment implications in the use of the GPS device." Supporters of his decision stress that GPS produces vital information in cases. For instance, they note, in 1999 it was used to follow a murder suspect to his victim's body, resulting in his conviction. As for concerns that officers may use GPS without discretion, Grable responds that police have neither the time nor the inclination to track people at random.

GPS and other innovations promise many advantages but often alarm privacy advocates. The following chapter offers competing analyses of technologies that may invite intrusions into Americans' personal lives. A key issue that emerges in this debate is whether privacy should be sacrificed for the convenience and security that technologies bring.

"The privacy practices and policies of commercial Web sites are continuing to evolve, and, by at least some criteria, to improve."

Internet Privacy Protections Have Improved

William F. Adkinson Jr., Jeffrey A. Eisenach, and Thomas M. Lenard

In the viewpoint that follows, William F. Adkinson Jr., Jeffrey A. Eisenach, and Thomas M. Lenard assert that the privacy protections of commercial Web sites have strengthened since 2000. A survey they commissioned found that Internet domains collect less personal information from visitors, and more allow consumers to decide how their information is used than they did in the past. Furthermore, the authors claim, fewer sites use cookies, which track Internet surfing across multiple Web sites. They also note that companies are actively helping marketers develop or update their online privacy policies. Lenard and Adkinson are senior staff members, and Eisenach is on the board of directors of the Progress and Freedom Foundation, a think tank which assesses the digital revolution.

As you read, consider the following questions:

1. According to the survey results, what percentage of the most popular Web sites and random sample Web sites utilize third-party cookies?
2. What offline sources mentioned by the authors produce enormous amounts of customer data?
3. Name three actions of PLI, as identified by the authors.

This study is the fourth in a series of surveys of the privacy practices of commercial sites on the Internet, dating back to 1998. It is designed to be directly comparable to the results from the most recent FTC [Federal Trade Commission] survey of Web sites, published in May 2000. The report also takes note of some of the major market-driven developments affecting the collection and use of personal information in the on-line environment.

PFF [the Progress & Freedom Foundation] engaged Ernst & Young to perform the survey, which was carried out in December 2001. The surfers surveyed three groups of domains, all selected based on estimates of traffic over sites provided by Nielsen/NetRatings: (1) the 85 busiest sites (the "Most Popular Group"), (2) a random sample of all of the sites with more than 39,000 unique visits (the "Random Sample"), and (3) a subset of the random sample restricted to the top 5,625 sites (the "Refined Random Sample").

Improvements in Privacy Protections

The survey revealed a continuing evolution in the privacy practices and policies of commercial Web sites. Among the most interesting findings:

- *Web sites are collecting less information.* Perhaps the most unexpected finding was that commercial Web sites are collecting less information than they were two years ago [in 2000]. Among the most popular domains, for example, the proportion collecting Personally Identifying Information ("PII") other than email fell from 96 percent to 84 percent; it fell from 87 percent to 74 percent for sites in the Random Sample. By every relevant measure, the extent of online information collection has declined since May 2000.

- *Fewer Web sites utilize third-party cookies.*[1] Cookies set by a Web site other than the one a user is visiting are called third-party cookies. Another form of information collection, the use of third-party cookies to track surfing behavior across multiple Web sites, is also down significantly. The proportion of Web sites that utilize third-party cookies fell from 78 percent to 48 percent for the most popular group and from 57 percent to 25 percent for the Random Sample.

- *Privacy notices are more prevalent, more prominent and more complete.* Practically all of the most popular domains and 83 percent of the Random Sample sites provide some privacy disclosure, little changed from 2000. However, substantially more of the random sample domains provide a privacy policy comprehensively stating how they handle consumer information. Overall, privacy notices tended to provide more information and were more likely to be accessible from a site's home page.

- *In general, consumers have more opportunities to choose how PII is used.* For example, the percentage of the most popular sites that offer choice over sharing consumer information with third parties—a key consumer concern—jumped from 77 percent to 93 percent. By contrast, there was little change in the availability of choice for internal use of PII (i.e. use by the Web site operator to send further communications), though such choice continues to be offered by 71 percent of sites in

---

1. A cookie is a file created by a Web site to store a user's preferences and any personal information they have disclosed.

the random sample and 89 percent of sites in the most popular group.

- *More sites offer opt-in; fewer offer opt-out.*[2] For choice over third-party use, opt-in more than doubled from 15 percent to 32 percent among the most popular domains, while opt-out fell from 49 percent to 30 percent. In the Random Sample opt-in increased from 11 percent to 18 percent, while opt-out declined from 59 percent to 53 percent.

- *More sites offer a combination of fair information practice elements.* The proportion of Web sites that provide a combination of notice, modified choice[3] and security [against unauthorized use of personal information] has increased both among the Random Sample and the Most Popular domains. Most striking is the fact that 80 percent of the most popular domains now provide all three elements, up from 63 percent in the 2000 survey.

- *P3P adoption is off to a rapid start, but adoption of seal programs [which identify sites that meet privacy standards]*[4] *is growing relatively slowly.* Although P3P enabled browsers were only available in late summer [2001], and the adoption of the standard is not yet final, one-quarter of the most popular domains and five percent of the random sample domains have already implemented this technology. Privacy seal programs, on the other hand, do not appear to be making major strides: the proportion of random-sample sites display-

2. Opt-out means that users must take further action to prevent their personal information from being used or shared with others. Opt-in means they must take action only if they want their information to be shared.

3. In other words, asking users if they want their information to be used internally, or shared with third parties.

4. The Platform for Privacy Preferences Project (P3P) is technology that automatically compares a user's privacy preferences to a Web site's privacy policy and notifies the user if the two are not compatible.

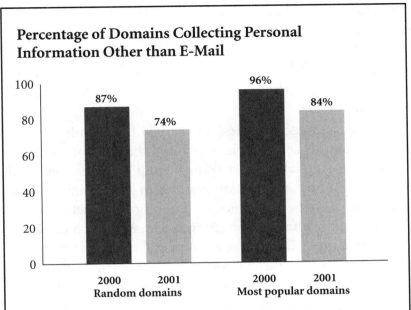

Percentage of Domains Collecting Personal Information Other than E-Mail

SOURCE: William F. Adkinson Jr., Jeffrey A. Eisenbach, and Thomas M. Lenard, *Privacy Online: A Report on the Information Practices and Policies of Commercial Web Sites*, Progress and Freedom Foundation, March 2002.

ing seals increased from eight percent to 12 percent, while the proportion in the most popular group was essentially unchanged.

What these results suggest, simply put, is that the privacy practices and policies of commercial Web sites are continuing to evolve, and, by at least some criteria, to improve. And, notably, some of the most significant changes are in the areas that have been identified as raising the greatest concerns for consumers—such as placement of third-party cookies and third party sharing of information.

Collection of Consumer Data

The digital revolution and the rise of the Internet have opened up important new ways for people to obtain information, interact and do business with each other. Indeed, e-commerce is one of the most important applications of the new communications technologies. Consumers can now research and compare products and make purchases from their home or workplace, obtaining far more information more quickly than they ever could before.

These same technologies [in the words of Paul H. Rubin and Thomas M. Lenard], "have reduced the costs of gathering, storing, manipulating and transmitting information of all kinds," including information relating to the commercial behavior of consumers. Neither the collection of such information nor its use to facilitate targeted marketing and related practices is new. Enormous amounts of consumer data have long been available through offline sources such as credit card transactions, phone orders, warranty cards, applications and a host of other traditional methods. What the digital revolution has done is increase the efficiency and effectiveness with which such information can be collected and put to use. Online collection of information—the main topic of this report—is thus only one aspect of a larger phenomenon.

Privacy Concerns

While there is little substantive difference between the nature and use of information collected in the online environment and information collected through more traditional means, consumers clearly are concerned about information collection by commercial Web sites. . . .

Many surveys have reported consumers' concerns about the potential abuse of the personal information they provide in the course of conducting transactions online. The FTC's May 2000 report cited consumer surveys indicating high levels of concern about the need for notice and choice, and practices such as the sharing of information with third-parties. Other experts caution against relying too heavily on indications of consumer concerns portrayed in consumer surveys, pointing out that whatever concerns consumers may have, online commerce continues to grow rapidly. Such polls have often produced surprising results—for example, that relatively few consumers actually read privacy notices. Indeed, a recent HarrisInteractive Poll found that only three percent of consumers read policies most of the time, and two-thirds spent little or any time looking at privacy policies.

Market Responses

Whatever one believes about the validity of polling data on consumer privacy, businesses operating in the online environment appear to be treating consumer concerns seriously. Accordingly, there have been a number of market responses to such concerns, in addition to those reflected in this survey. For example, the Privacy Leadership Initiative (PLI), a partnership of CEOs from major corporations and leading business associations, has instituted a number of programs aimed both at businesses and consumers. In February 2002, if partnered with the Chamber of Commerce to offer "Privacy Made Simple," a free online resource with tools and information that small to medium-sized businesses can use to develop or upgrade their privacy policies and notices. It plans to partner with other business associations who can aid their efforts to reach medium and small businesses. PLI is also promoting the development of software to make developing and implementing privacy policies easier for small businesses. For consumers, PLI engages in extensive consumer education efforts through banner ad and radio campaigns. Together with the Internet Education Foundation, it also provides an online "consumer toolbox" offering information and links to software that can help consumers protect their information.

Industry is also supporting efforts to improve the effectiveness of privacy notices. PLI has funded extensive research by HarrisInteractive to better understand how to best provide useful notices to consumers. The Center for Information Policy

Leadership at Hunton & Williams [law firm] is developing a consumer-friendly template for privacy notices. Dubbed the "Short Notices Project," the goal is to create templates that can be widely used to provide short and simple notices consumers can understand, and "layer" the provision of information.

The Direct Marketing Association ("DMA") continues to make its Privacy Promise program a requirement for its business-to-consumer members. This program requires those members to provide customers the option of "opting out" of information exchanges as well as the option not to be recontacted, both in the offline and online context. The DMA recently adopted Online Information Guidelines setting forth how notice, choice and other fair practice principles should be implemented on members' Web sites. These Guidelines are enforceable through its Ethical Business Practice Committee. The Online Privacy Alliance has also supported a number of initiatives aimed at identifying effective approaches to privacy protection, aiding in the development and dissemination of technology tools to protect privacy, and promoting adoption of privacy programs and compliance with them.

Finally, industry is promoting technological research on privacy issues. In November 2001, for example, IBM announced the formation of the IBM Institute and the Privacy Management Council, dedicated to privacy and data protection technologies. The Council will include privacy experts from a range of industries who will collaborate with IBM to develop technologies designed to meet emerging privacy needs. And ... the Platform for Privacy Preferences empowers consumers to program their browsers to reflect their desired level of privacy protection and check the compatibility of a site's policies.

"Companies continually troll for, and exploit, personally identifiable . . . information on the internet."

Internet Privacy Is Imperiled

Joseph Turow

In the following viewpoint Joseph Turow, a professor at the University of Pennsylvania's Annenberg School for Communication, warns that Internet users are under constant surveillance. Internet domains, he explains, use cookies and other tracking methods to record consumers' surfing habits. Alarmingly, Web sites use this data to develop customer profiles, which they then sell to marketers, Turow avers. Unfortunately, many Internet surfers do not know how to prevent online companies from gathering information about them, Turow maintains, and they mistakenly believe that sites with privacy policies will not disclose their information to others.

As you read, consider the following questions:

1. What technologies are used to track people's e-mail and keyboard activities, as cited by the author?

Joseph Turow, *Americans and Online Privacy: The System Is Broken*, Annenberg Public Policy Center of the University of Pennsylvania, June 2003, pp. 3–7, 10, 16–19. Reproduced by permission.

2. In what way might consumer profiling lead to discrimination, according to Turow?

3. What conclusion does the author draw from the findings that 21 percent of people like to disclose their information to Web sites in exchange for offers and 16 percent give out their information only if paid?

This new national survey reveals that American adults who go online at home misunderstand the very purpose of privacy policies. The study is also the first to provide evidence that the overwhelming majority of U.S. adults who use the internet at home have no clue about data flows—the invisible, cutting edge techniques whereby online organizations extract, manipulate, append, profile and share information about them. Even if they have a sense that sites track them and collect individual bits of their data, they simply don't fathom how those bits can be used. In fact, when presented with a common way that sites currently handle consumers' information, they say they would not accept it. The findings suggest that years into attempts by governments and advocacy groups to educate people about internet privacy, the system is more broken than ever.

Privacy Violations

- 57% of U.S. adults who use the internet at home believe incorrectly that when a website has a privacy policy, it will not share their personal information with other websites or companies.

- 47% of U.S. adults who use the internet at home say website privacy policies are easy to understand. However, 66% of those who are confident about their understanding of privacy policies also believe (incorrectly) that sites with a privacy policy won't share data.

- 59% of adults who use the internet at home know that websites collect information about them even if they don't register. They do not, however, understand that data flows behind their screens invisibly connect[ing] seemingly unrelated bits about them. When presented with a common version of the way sites track, extract, and share information to make money from advertising, 85% of adults who go online at home did not agree to accept it on even a valued site. When offered a choice to get content from a valued site with such a policy or pay for the site and not have it collect information, 54% of adults who go online at home said that they would rather leave the web for that content than do either.

- Among the 85% who did not accept the policy, one in two (52%) had earlier said they gave or would likely give the valued site their real name and email address—the very information a site needs to begin creating a personally identifiable dataset about them.

- Despite strong concerns about online information privacy, 64% of these online adults say they have never searched for information about how to protect their information on the web; 40% say that they know "almost nothing" about stopping sites from collecting information about them, and 26% say they know just "a little." Only 9% of American adults who use the internet at home say they know a lot.

- Overwhelmingly, however, they support policies that make learning what online companies know about them straightforward. 86% believe that laws that force website policies to have a standard format will be effective in helping them protect their information. . . .

Companies Exploit Personal Information

With the exception of certain personal health information, certain types of personal financial information held by certain types of firms, and personally identifiable information from children younger than 13 years, online companies have virtually free reign to use individuals' data in the U.S. for business purposes without their knowledge or consent. They can take, utilize and share personally identifiable information—that is, information that they link to individuals' names and addresses. They can also create, package and sell detailed profiles of people whose names they do not know but whose interests and lifestyles they feel they can infer from their web-surfing activities.

Companies continually troll for, and exploit, personally identifiable and non-personally identifiable information on the internet. They often begin by getting the names and email addresses of people who sign up for web sites. They can then associate this basic information with a small text file called a cookie that can record the various activities that the registering individual has carried out online during that session and later sessions. Tracking with cookies is just the beginning, however. By using other technologies such as web bugs, spyware, chat-room analysis and transactional database software, web entities can follow people's email and keyboard activities and serve ads to them even when they are off-line. Moreover, companies can extend their knowledge of personally identifiable individuals by purchasing information about them from list firms off the web and linking the information to their own databases. That added knowledge allows them to send targeted editorial matter or advertising to consumers. More specificity also increases the value of the databases when they are marketed to other interested data-trollers.

Marketing to Marketers

Marketers and media firms use consumer information in a broad gamut of ways and with varying concerns for how far the data travel. Some websites unabashedly collect all the information they can about visitors and market them as aggressively as they can to advertisers and other marketers. Though many of these emphasize personally identifiable information, not all of them do. Tracking people anonymously can still lead to useful targeting. An important example is the Gator Corporation, which places its tracking files into people's computers when they download free software such as the KaZaA music-sharing program.

The company claims to be in 35 million computers and says that once there, "The Gator Corporation has the ability to ride along with consumers as they surf the Web. That allows us to display targeted ads based on actual behavior and deliver incredible insights." A pitch to potential clients continues:

> Here's an example: Gator knows this consumer is a new parent based on their real-time and historical online behavior—looking for information on childbirth, looking for baby names, shopping for baby products. . . .
>
> Let's say you sell baby food. We know which consumers are displaying behaviors relevant to the baby food category through their online behavior. Instead of targeting primarily by demographics, you can target consumers who are showing or have shown an interest in your category. . . .
>
> *Joseph Turow,* Americans and Online Privacy: The System Is Broken, *Annenberg Public Policy Center of the University of Pennsylvania, June 2003.*

Discriminatory and Disrespectful

The invisible nature of much of the tracking and sorting can lead marketers to make generalizations about consumers that the consumers don't know and don't agree with. Inferences drawn from demographics and web-surfing habits can encourage discrimination in the kinds of editorial and advertising materials a site shows consumers. Such activities will become more intense as technologies to mine data, analyze data, and tailor based on the conclusions become more efficient and cost-effective. As they expand, the activities may well lead people to feel anxious not only that they are being tracked but that they are being treated differently—for example, given different discounts—than others because of who they are and what their "clickstream" says about them.

Law professor Jeffrey Rosen poses the humanistic critique bluntly. Paraphrasing the Czech writer Milan Kundera, he suggests that "by requiring citizens to live in glass houses without curtains, totalitarian societies deny their status as individuals." He goes on to note that spying on people without their knowledge is an indignity: "It fails to treat its objects as fully deserving of respect, and treats them instead like animals in a zoo, deceiving them about the nature of their own surroundings." . . .

The Drawbacks of P3P

A bold technological solution that has gained industry traction during the past few years is the Platform for Privacy Preferences (P3P). Its goal is to provide a web-wide computer-readable standard manner for websites to communicate their privacy policies automatically to people's computers. In that way visitors can know immediately when they get to a site whether they feel comfortable with its information policy. A recent report by an AT&T Labs group found that while P3P's adoption by websites is growing, especially on the most popular sites, fewer than 10% of websites offer it.

One reason that sites eschew P3P is that it requires them to transform their privacy policies into a number of straightforward answers to multiple choice questions. P3P consequently does not allow for the ambiguities, evasions and legal disclaimers that are hallmarks of such documents. Note, too, that the P3P approach does not have a facility for ensuring that websites answer the questions accurately or truthfully. . . .

Americans and Internet Privacy

Beyond reflecting concerns about outsiders invading their privacy, the pattern of answers are a springboard to . . . themes that speak to the major questions posed earlier:

- *The great majority of adults who go online at home reject the general proposition that their information is a currency for commercial barter.* Only 21% agree that they like to give information to websites in exchange for offers, and only 16% agree that they will give out information only if paid. The answers mirror responses by [parents surveyed] in 2000. They contradict analysts who characterize most Americans as quite open to giving up their information if the price is right. Philosophically, if not always in practice, adults who use the web at home do not see their personal information as a commodity to be traded for online offers.

- *Most adults who go online at home know that websites track their behavior, but two in five are ignorant about the most basic aspect of information collection on the internet.* 59% are aware of what cookies do; they know that when they go online sites collect information on them even if they don't register. The flip side of the finding is that 40% of U.S. adults who use the internet at home are not aware of this most basic way that companies track their actions when they go online. Yet 76% of them say that "they look to see if a website has a privacy policy before answering any questions." In addition, 69% say they "always" or "sometimes" give their real email address to a website when it asks for personal information. Because privacy policies almost always mention cookies, the answers suggest that even though these people say they "look to see if a website has a privacy policy," the great proportion of online adults who aren't aware of what cookies do either don't actually read the policies or don't understand them.

- *The attitude statements also reveal that beyond being nervous over their sense of being tracked, most Americans want help to control their information.* 95% agree that they should have a legal right to know everything a website knows about them. . . .

Despite strong concerns about government and corporate intrusions, American adults who use the internet at home don't understand the flow of their data online. Our survey reveals a disconnect between their concern about information about them online and their knowledge about what websites do with it.

> "*Limits need to be placed on [closed-circuit television] surveillance to ensure that privacy and anonymity is protected in public.*"

Public Video Surveillance Is Intrusive

Benjamin J. Goold

In the following viewpoint Benjamin J. Goold argues that closed-circuit television cameras that record activity in public places invade people's privacy. He emphasizes that public interactions are governed by conventions of anonymity. Being anonymous, he explains, allows people to maintain a sense of dignity and autonomy while in public and to choose how to respond to those around them. When people are watched over a camera, however, they lose their anonymity, Goold points out. Worse, they are exposed to prolonged scrutiny from unknown observers with unidentified intentions, he maintains. Goold is an adjunct professor at John Jay College of Criminal Justice in New York.

As you read, consider the following questions:

Benjamin J. Goold, "Privacy Rights and Public Spaces: CCTV and the Problem of the Unobservable Observer," *Criminal Justice Ethics*, vol. 21, Winter-Spring 2002, p. 21. Copyright 2002 Institute of Criminal Justice Ethics. Reproduced by permission.

1. In Goold's opinion, in what way are privacy rights essential to personal autonomy?
2. According to von Hirsch, what kind of observation is seen as inappropriate and unacceptable?
3. Why is it important for a person to see his or her observer, in the author's contention?

[Since 1992,] closed circuit television (CCTV) cameras have become an increasingly familiar part of the urban landscape in many developed countries. Throughout Europe, despite early concerns about the possible implications for human rights, governments have now begun to regard video surveillance technology as a "magic bullet" in the fight against crime and public disorder. In Britain alone, over one million cameras have been installed in towns and cities across the country, with an estimated 500 being added to this number every week.

Unregulated Surveillance

While initially slow to embrace this new technology, in recent years public area CCTV has also begun to become more popular in the United States. Street cameras can now be found in Boston, Los Angeles, and New York as well as in a growing number of smaller cities and towns. In many instances, these cameras have been installed without public consent or even public discussion and are subject to little in the way of either formal or informal legal regulation. Provided they have the support of local government, the police and other law enforcement agencies are free to monitor public spaces such as streets, parks, and open malls with little regard for the concerns of private citizens.

To some extent, this lack of regulation stems from a reluctance on the part of the courts to tackle the question of whether individuals have some legitimate expectation of privacy in public spaces. . . .

Whether we like it or not, public area surveillance technology is now a fact of life, and there is a pressing need for us to reconsider many of our assumptions—legal and ethical—about the nature and importance of privacy rights.

Privacy as a Civil Liberty

Although there are many competing conceptions of privacy as a civil liberty, one of the most coherent accounts is that advanced by the legal philosopher David Feldman. According to Feldman, privacy rights are important because they provide individuals with the ability to determine and control the boundaries between different, interlocking social spheres. For most of us, our daily lives are lived in a number of social contexts, many of which may overlap. At home I am a husband, at work a teacher, and at my local sports club a member of a team. In each case, I assume different responsibilities, respond to different expectations, and maintain different levels of intimacy with those around me. Privacy conventions enable me to exert varying degrees of control over the borders between these different spheres and to limit the extent to which I am subject to the demands of others within them. While I do not abandon my identity as a husband when I leave home every morning, I am not obliged to reveal details about my marriage to my employer, my students, or some stranger I meet on the street. Equally, even in my own home and surrounded by those closest to me, there may be certain thoughts that I choose to keep to myself and certain activities that I prefer to engage in alone. In this regard, privacy is a matter of being able to choose how I respond to the demands and curiosity of those around me and of maintaining some degree of control over how I present myself to the world.

Within this framework, privacy rights deserve protection because they are essential for the maintenance of personal autonomy and because they enable individuals to maintain a range of different and valuable social relationships. If we are

Video Surveillance Has a Chilling Effect on Public Life

The growing presence of public cameras will bring subtle but profound changes to the character of our public spaces. When citizens are being watched by the authorities—or aware they might be watched at any time—they are more self-conscious and less free-wheeling. As syndicated columnist Jacob Sullum has pointed out, "knowing that you are being watched by armed government agents tends to put a damper on things. You don't want to offend them or otherwise call attention to yourself." Eventually, he warns, "people may learn to be careful about the books and periodicals they read in public, avoiding titles that might alarm unseen observers. They may also put more thought into how they dress, lest they look like terrorists, gang members, druggies or hookers." Indeed, the studies of cameras in Britain found that people deemed to be "out of time and place" with the surroundings were subjected to prolonged surveillance.

American Civil Liberties Union, "What's Wrong with Public Video Surveillance?" February 25, 2002.

constantly having to respond to the expectations of those around us, our choices are unlikely ever to be free, and we are unlikely to develop a capacity for self-determination or a degree of self-fulfillment. . . .

The Importance of Anonymity

In attempting to identify what sorts of privacy interests are at stake in public spaces—and what these interests might look like—it is useful to begin by examining some of the informal, everyday conventions that govern social interactions in public.

Clearly, when it comes to watching others in public, certain forms of observation are regarded as being inherently more intrusive than others. As [criminal law expert Andrew] von Hirsch has noted, while most people expect to be the subject of "casual and momentary" observation, anything more is likely to be seen as somehow inappropriate and unacceptable. When I walk down the street or through a crowded park, for example, I expect to be noticed by those around me. I do not expect, however, to be stared at intently, followed, or subjected to some other special or prolonged scrutiny, unless I am doing something out of the ordinary or attempting to draw particular attention to myself. Furthermore, being able to see who is watching me is also important. I can only choose how to respond to more than casual or momentary observation if I am aware of being observed.

According to von Hirsch, these "conventions of anonymity" exist to ensure that individuals are able to go about in public without being identified or feeling the need to respond to the curiosity and expectations of strangers. In this regard, they provide us with a modicum of personal privacy and help us to maintain a sense of dignity and autonomy as we go about our lives in public. In terms of the general framework outlined by Feldman, it follows then that privacy rights should be extended to public spaces insofar as they serve to protect an individual's legitimate expectations of anonymity.

Having established a connection between anonymity expectations and privacy interests, von Hirsch goes on to argue that CCTV surveillance violates these identified conventions by exposing individuals to the possibility of prolonged scrutiny from unobservable observers. As he points out, CCTV surveillance necessarily involves camera operators zooming in on and following individuals even if they are not doing anything in particular to draw attention to themselves. Furthermore, regardless of whether CCTV cameras are obvious or covert, it is unlikely that the persons under surveillance are going to be aware that they are being watched. [von Hirsch notes:]

> Often, the presence of CCTV is unannounced, and the cameras are concealed. But even if the cameras are unconcealed, the fact that they are mechanical, positioned above people's line of vision, and blend in with other features of the physical environment makes them easily overlooked. A camera is likely to be ignored in a way that a police officer is not.

According to von Hirsch, limits need to be placed on the use of CCTV surveillance to ensure that privacy and anonymity is protected in public spaces. . . .

The Problem of the Unobservable Observer

Von Hirsch is right when he suggests that part of the problem lies with the fact we do not know who is operating the camera or what they are looking for. Being able to identify who is watching us is crucial if we are to be able to make decisions about how to adjust our behavior (or not) in the light of such observation. But placing a bar on covert surveillance, as suggested by von Hirsch, provides only a partial solution to the problem (something he himself acknowledges). Knowing that we are being watched by a camera is not the same as knowing the identity of who is watching us. All that we know is that we are being watched, but it is impossible for us to know why or by whom. This is the reason that we draw a distinction between being watched by a visible police officer and a CCTV camera mounted on the side of the building. Seeing, identifying, and attempting to understand the motives of whoever is watching us is an essential precursor to deciding how we feel about being observed and to deciding how to respond to such observation.

Take for example the case of being watched in public by two strangers, one a small girl and the other a man wearing a dark suit and sunglasses. Even if both watch from the same distance and for the same length of time, they are most likely to evoke different responses. In the case of the child, most people would assume that the girl's motive for paying such close attention to them is either benign or unimportant. In the case of the stranger in sunglasses, however, we may be less certain that his reason for watching us is benevolent. Being able to see each of them—the girl and the man in sunglasses— is, however, crucial to the drawing of these conclusions. Once we are able to see and to know something about the identity of the observer, we are then in a position to draw inferences from their appearance and behavior about their possible motives for watching us. I may, of course, be wrong in my estimations. The small child might be watching with the intention of doing me some harm while the man in sunglasses may simply be especially curious. Given, however, that what matters—at least as far as my immediate privacy interests are concerned—is how being observed makes me feel, in a sense it is not important whether I have come to the right conclusions in either case. What matters is whether being able to draw these inferences has made me more comfortable with the fact of being observed and that conventions of anonymity have been violated.

Even when they are clearly visible and obvious, however, CCTV cameras deny us the possibility of drawing such conclusions. Instead, we are left to wonder exactly who is watching us and for what reason. Although I may suspect that I am being monitored for signs of criminal behavior, because there is no way of knowing who is controlling the camera or watching my image, there is also no way for me to confirm that my assumption is correct. Perhaps no one is watching, or I am being watched by dozens of people who have no business looking at me at all. Perhaps I am being watched by a highly trained, professional camera operator bound by clear ethical standards or by a voyeuristic pervert and ten of his friends who have just dropped into the control room for an afternoon of entertainment. Unable to see my watchers, I cannot know for certain which is the case and, therefore, how I feel about being watched.

"*Video cameras in public places do not physically intrude into a person's sphere of privacy.*"

Public Video Surveillance Is Not Intrusive

Gus Arroyo

Gus Arroyo is a lieutenant at the Fremont Police Department in California. He contends in the following viewpoint that video cameras in public places deter crime while only minimally violating privacy. He asserts that video surveillance enjoys popular support as well as legal protections. According to Arroyo, U.S. courts have ruled that people out in public generally do not have a reasonable expectation of privacy; therefore, videotaping citizens does not usually violate their privacy rights. Video monitoring is no different, he claims, than police officers who wait in an area to watch for crime.

As you read, consider the following questions:

1. What resulted from the installation of sixty video cameras in King's Lynn, according to Arroyo?

Gus Arroyo, "The Impact of Video Monitoring Technology on Police Field Operations," *Police Futurists International*, November 22, 2002. Reproduced by permission.

2. What are the two parts of the Katz test, as cited by the author?

3. In the author's assertion, what has California tort law determined regarding video monitoring of public places?

For many years now video monitoring systems have been used by the private sector to enhance security operations in banks, casinos, convenience stores, offices, private residences and many other commercial and retail establishments. . . . The proliferation of video cameras has been real and its continuation is almost certain. One need only look around while driving a vehicle to spot video cameras monitoring activity in various locations of America's towns, cities, and highways. The number of privately owned video cameras monitoring activity in the United States is unknown but their popularity as a crime prevention tool has attracted the attention of law enforcement agencies, and many are jumping on the video monitoring technology train.

Using Video Surveillance to Nab Criminals

In Britain, the use of Closed Circuit Television (CCTV) cameras has become an integral part of that government's crime control policy, social control theory and community consciousness. British police and politicians promote video monitoring as the primary solution for urban dysfunction and credit video monitoring technology for having had more impact in the evolution of law enforcement policy than any other technology in the past two decades.

In a work titled "The Transparent Society" David Brin [a scientist and science fiction author] wrote:

The trend began in Britain a decade ago, in the city of King's Lynn, where sixty remote controlled video cameras were installed to scan known "trouble spots," reporting directly to police headquarters. The resulting reduction in street crime exceeded all predictions; in or near zones covered by surveillance, it dropped to one seventieth of the former amount. The savings in patrol costs alone paid for the equipment in a few months. Dozens of cities and towns soon followed the example of King's Lynn. Glasgow, Scotland, reported a 68% drop in citywide crime, while police in Newcastle fingered over 1500 perpetrators with taped evidence. (All but seven pleaded guilty, and those seven were later convicted.) In May 1997, a thousand Newcastle soccer fans rampaged through downtown streets. Detectives studying the video reels picked out 152 faces and published eighty photos in local newspapers. In days all were identified.

Support for police use of video monitoring technology in the United States has not reached the same level as in Britain, considered the leader in the use of CCTV, but there are indications that support is growing. Even before the terrorist attacks of September 11, 2001, police cameras monitored public areas in a number of U.S. cities. In-Car Mobile Video cameras, Red Light Photo Enforcement cameras, portable Cams, and CCTV cameras have in fact become common and are widely accepted. The private use of video monitoring systems is even more pervasive. By some estimates, in 2001, over 200,000 video lookouts were in place and monitoring in and around private homes. One such camera helped catch a suspected killer and rapist in Sacramento, California. The camera, which cost $2,400, was purchased by 10 neighbors and was installed by one of them to monitor their court.

Video Monitoring as a Crime Deterrent

Although hotly debated, there appears to be a general perception that video monitoring technology helps to deter crime. Critics contend that there is no evidence to support such a claim and that video monitoring by police brings communities closer to [1984 author] George Orwell's nightmare of Big Brother [a government surveillance state]. Proponents argue that the vast majority of video monitoring systems are privately owned and not government controlled and that even those that are government owned and operated do not appear to be used for the repressive purposes Orwell warned about. Even some opponents have found that there is general public acceptance of the use of video monitoring technology by law enforcement for purposes of crime prevention. In "A Cautionary Tale for a New Age of Surveillance", [legal expert] Jeffery Rosen wrote:

> Instead of being perceived as an Orwellian intrusion, the cameras in Britain proved to be extremely popular. They were hailed as the people's technology, a friendly eye in the sky, not Big Brother at all but a kindly and watchful uncle or aunt. Local governments could not get enough of them; each hamlet and fen in the British countryside wanted its own CCTV surveillance system, even when the most serious threat to public safety was coming from mad cows. In 1994, 79 city centers had surveillance networks; by 1998, 440 city centers were wired. By the late 1990s, as part of its Clintonian, center-left campaign to be tough on crime, Tony Blair's New Labor government decided to support the cameras with a vengeance. There are now so many cameras attached to so many different surveillance systems in the U.K. that people have stopped counting. According to some estimates there are 2.5 million surveillance cameras in Britain, and in fact there may be far more.

In his forward to a publication of the Constitution of the United States, Warren Burger, Chief Justice of the United States, wrote, "Ever since people began living in tribes and villages, they have had to balance order with liberty. Individual freedom had to be weighed against the need for security of all". The challenge to find the right balance has today perhaps been made more difficult by technologies like video monitoring. Yet, no one more than government, and law enforcement in particular, has the duty and responsibility to achieve that balance. The power of video monitoring technology is great and therefore the potential for abusing it is great. While the courts will ultimately decide which law enforcement uses of

The Benefits of Video Monitoring Far Surpass the Risks

For years, privacy advocates have raised warnings about the risks and costs of putting streets, subway stations and other sites under constant electronic monitoring. . . .

But when the [video surveillance] cameras help to catch terrorists bent on mass slaughter, the civil liberties complaints suddenly sound pathetically trivial.

Stephen Chapman, Conservative Chronicle, *July 28, 2005.*

video monitoring technology are acceptable and which are not, as the public servants tasked with maintaining order, law enforcement must guard against being overzealous in the use of video monitoring technology and tipping the scale completely against individual freedom.

Legal Considerations

Most legal analysts have concluded that the use of video technology to monitor public places is permitted and does not present significant legal obstacles. Although the courts have not addressed the issue directly, there is significant case law on closely related issues to support this position. In a Public Law Research Institute study that considered the impact of the First and Fourth Amendments of the United States Constitution, federal statutory law, specifically the Electronics Communications Privacy Act, and California tort law on the legality of continuous video surveillance, Scott Sher concluded:

> Continuous video surveillance does not implicate First Amendment, Fourth Amendment, or tort law concerns. Even though courts have not addressed the precise question as to

whether or not continuous video surveillance would survive legal scrutiny, past Supreme Court and lower court decisions strongly suggest that this type of police monitoring is a valid exercise of a state's police powers.

While the monitoring of public places using video technology has been determined to be legal, it is not totally without restrictions. In *Katz v. United States* [1967], the Supreme Court declared that "the Fourth Amendment protects people not places." The court further added, "What a person knowingly exposes to the public, even in his own home or office is not subject to Fourth Amendment protection," but, "what he (that person) seeks to preserve as private, even in an area accessible to the public may be constitutionally protected." In an effort to balance the privacy interests of individuals and society's desire to maintain effective law enforcement, the court adopted a two-part test. Known as the Katz test, it asks the following two questions, "(1) Has the individual manifested a subjective expectation of privacy? and, (2) Is society prepared to recognize that expectation as reasonable and legitimate?"

Based on this test, the prevailing opinion is that individuals have no reasonable expectation of privacy on public streets from visual observation, including video monitoring cameras. However, the use of cameras that rotate and have superior visual enhancing capabilities able to capture activity in private property from afar do not always satisfy the Katz test and may violate Fourth Amendment protections. In "Future Imperfect", Dr. David D. Friedman observed:

> Few would consider it objectionable to have a police officer wandering a park or standing on a street corner keeping an eye out for purse snatchers and the like. Video cameras on poles are simply a more convenient way of doing the same thing—comfortably and out of the wet. Cameras at red lights, or photometric monitoring of a car's exhaust plume,

are merely cheaper and more effective substitutes for traffic cops and emission inspectors.

The problem comes when this video monitoring technology is combined with other technologies, such as biometric facial recognition, thermal sensing, infrared, and others that greatly enhance human visual capabilities. As Dr. Friedman added, "Some technologies make the job of law enforcement harder. Others make it easier—even too easy." The use of cameras with audio recording capabilities that capture sound may also violate Title 1 of the Electronic Communications Privacy Act. Title 1 prohibits the intentional interception or attempted interception of any wire, oral, or electronic communication without a warrant. Title 1 does not restrict the use of silent video monitoring cameras that do not capture audio signals.

In California the courts have recognized privacy under tort law [which is a branch of civil law]. But most legal scholars have concluded that video cameras in public places do not physically intrude into a person's sphere of privacy, and any invasion of privacy caused by them is minimal. Thus the use of video cameras to monitor public places has been considered permissible and not liable under California tort law. In short, most legal scholars agree that past court decisions suggest the use of video monitoring technology is allowed, within certain limitations, as a valid exercise of a state's police powers to provide for the safety of a community.

Social Implications

The use of video technology by law enforcement, even if determined to be legal, carries some far-reaching social implications. Americans pride themselves in having the world's most free society and have come to expect both security and liberty, not one over the other. . . .

Will the use of this technology make officers and citizens feel safer and more secure? Or will it only make them distrusting and induce them to social conformity only because they can't be sure when they are being watched? David Brin argues that the effectiveness of modern video monitoring technology as a crime prevention and investigative tool makes privacy no longer an option. He proposes as an alternative to privacy universal lack of privacy—the transparent society. In Brin's transparent society not only would the community be safer and more secure from criminals they would also be safer and more secure from police misconduct.

"*The implementation of biometrics will have disproportionate effects on privacy and civil liberties.*"

Biometric Travel Documents Threaten Privacy

Privacy International and the American Civil Liberties Union

To enhance security, the International Civil Aviation Organization (ICAO) has proposed that passports and other travel documents contain passengers' biometric information—fingerprints, iris scans, and/or photographs. The information could then be run through a central database to verify the identity of the travelers and identify any terrorists or criminals. The following viewpoint is excerpted from a letter to the ICAO penned by Privacy International and the American Civil Liberties Union and signed by dozens of other rights organizations. The groups caution that maintaining national databases of such sensitive data could lead to surveillance, tracking, and profiling of citizens.

As you read, consider the following questions:

1. According to Privacy International and the ACLU, the

ICAO's policies infringe on rights set forth in what international agreements?

2. In the authors' contention, biometrics is a fallible technology that will produce what three results?

3. What is the authors' objection to RFID-tagged passports?

To the participants of the International Civil Aviation Organization [ICAO] 12th Session of the Facilitation Division,

We are writing to you on behalf of a wide range of human rights and civil liberties organizations to express our concerns regarding a number of decisions emerging from your conferences and their likely effects on privacy and civil liberties. We are particularly worried about your plans requiring passports and other travel documents to contain biometrics and remotely readable 'contact-less integrated circuits' [computer chips containing personal data].

We are increasingly concerned that the biometric travel document initiative is part and parcel of a larger surveillance infrastructure monitoring the movement of individuals globally that includes Passenger-Name Record transfers, API [Advance Passenger Information] systems, and the creation of an intergovernmental network of interoperable electronic data systems to facilitate access to each country's law enforcement and intelligence information.

We are concerned that the ICAO is setting a surveillance standard for the rest of the world to follow. In this sense, the ICAO is setting domestic policy, implementing profiling and ID cards where previously none may have existed, or enhancing ID documentation through the use of biometrics, and increasing the data pouring into national databases, or creating them when none previously existed.

While we understand the desire of the ICAO to increase confidence in travel documents, reduce fraud, combat terrorism, and protect aviation security, the implementation of biometrics will have disproportionate effects on privacy and civil liberties: These rights are enshrined in a number of international conventions and treaties including article 12 of the United Nations Declaration of Human Rights, Article 17 of the International Covenant on Civil and Political Rights, Article 8 of the European Convention for the Protection of Human Rights and Fundamental Freedoms, and a number of national constitutions and legal systems. The actions of the ICAO threaten these rights.

Protecting the Privacy of Movement

The right to movement is viewed as a fundamental right around the world, akin to the right to assemble. Border and aviation security necessarily involves scrutinising travellers and the use of personal information, but in light of the fundamental human rights involved, must be approached with the utmost thought and care. The ICAO's biometrics-based approach to securing travel documents unfortunately does not reflect such care—in fact, it is enabling the creation of a global surveillance infrastructure.

Concern about biometric travel documents is high around the world, and has been recognized even by many national governments:

- The U.S. Department of Homeland Security and the Department of State note that privacy issues need to be resolved prior to the implementation of these systems.

- Even as the European Commission has advocated a centralised database solution, storing the biometrics of all EU [European Union] travel document holders, it has noted that further research is necessary to "examine the impact of the establishment of such a European Register on the fundamental rights of European citizens, and in particular their right to data protection."

- The French Government has concluded similarly, requiring that any implementation of biometric techniques is systematically subject to prior agreement from its national privacy commission.

- As ICAO has itself noted, some States are legally barred from storing biometrics.

Avoiding National Biometric Databases

Because they are not carefully crafted, the ICAO standards risk ignoring these international warnings, resulting in the creation of centralized national databases of personal biometric information.

The European Union, for example, is already using the call for biometric passports to propose the establishment of a central European store of fingerprints, which would enable national databases, national-ID cards, and background searches. The EU is also calling for storage capacity on the chips contained in its passports to be significantly larger than the ICAO standard of 32K, thus allowing for additional information to be included in the future enabling further function creep.

Central databases become privacy risks through the disclosure of personal information, through the challenges of securing such large data stores, and through the use of biometric data for other purposes. Additionally, the centralised storage of biometric data increases the risk of the use of biometric data as a key to interconnecting databases that, according to EU privacy officials "could lead to detailed profiles of an individual's habits both in the public and in the private sector."

Such databases will also lead to the increased transfer of personal information across borders as individuals travel. When an EU citizen's identity is verified in the U.S., for example, will the American authorities download the facial and fingerprint data from the EU databases, or will U.S. authorities retain the biometric data they collect when verifying the document, along with other similar data for the next 50 years?

The Threats Posed by Biometrics

Face-recognition cameras are now common at airports, on city streets, and in other public places. Biometric technologies also include retina or iris scanners, digitized fingerprints and handprints, and voiceprints. They even include implantable rice-sized radio frequency chips coded with personal information that can be displayed by a scanner. . . .

No one wants to be treated like a human bar code by the authorities. . . .

The most-pressing threat to liberty is the first, all-inclusive database mandated by government—a national identification card with biometric identifiers. The threat of such an ID is apparent—it is involuntary, will increase unwelcome surveillance, and will undercut a presumptive right to maintain anonymity. It would devolve into a general law enforcement tool having nothing to do with the terrorism that prompted recent calls for national IDs, and would blur the distinction between public and private databases.

A less-sweeping biometric database would be partial, containing criminals and suspects, but not the general population, such as face-recognition cameras deployed in public places like airports and sporting events. Individuals would be observed, but presumably only to see if they matched a face already in the database by way of proper legal procedures. Nevertheless, many observers doubt that governments can be trusted to discard incidental data collected on innocents. . . .

The challenge of the biometric future is to prevent mandatory national ID cards, ensure Fourth Amendment protections with respect to public surveillance, and avoid the blurring of public and private databases.

Clyde Wayne Crews Jr., USA Today (Magazine), *July 2003.*

Similarly, when citizens of other countries visit EU member states, will they be required to submit fingerprints even though the ICAO travel documentation standards do not require fingerprint data? Until these questions are resolved, no standards for interoperability should be established at the ICAO.

Already there is some discussion of sharing biometric information with private companies. Airline check-in procedures will involve verifying the integrity of the travel documents, and airlines may retain the biometrics data. As part of the Advance Passenger Information systems,[1] some foresee the biometric information also being transferred by airlines to government agencies at passengers' destinations.

Face Recognition Technology

Biometrics is a fallible technology that will increase surveillance, erroneously subject individuals to undue attention, and, unless implemented carefully, will lead to increased collection and processing of data and transfer across borders.

The ICAO's choice of facial recognition [technology] as the standard remains problematic:

- Facial recognition contains a high likelihood of false non-matches (where valid individuals are refused border entry because the technology fails to recognise them), and false matches (where an individual is matched to another individual incorrectly). The ICAO standards do not govern the use to which the facial recognition data is put, but even the most reliable uses of this technology—one-to-one verification using recent photographs—have been shown in U.S. government tests to be highly unreliable, returning a false non-match rate of 5 percent and a false match rate of 1 percent.

---

1. These systems capture and analyze data on passengers' travel documents before the travellers arrive at their destinations.

- Furthermore, the reliability rates quickly deteriorated as photographs went out of date, climbing to 15 per cent after only about 2 years for the best systems tested. For governments that use the data to perform more ambitious one-to-many searches, tests show that the error rates would be sharply higher still.

- Implementation of facial recognition on a global scale is likely to increase these errors, and will lead to delays, duress, and confusion.

- Facial recognition technologies may reveal racial or ethnic origin.

- The U.S. General Accounting Office warns that facial recognition is the only biometric that can be used for other surveillance applications, such as pinpointing individuals filmed on video cameras.

Invasive Technologies Must Be Reassessed

We are very concerned that the [ICAO's] New Orleans resolution permits individual countries to use multiple biometrics, such as iris scans and fingerprints *in addition to* facial recognition. These additional physical measures increase the likelihood that biometric databases will be used for other purposes. The New Orleans resolution is contrary to your stated goal of interoperability and allows countries to pursue invasive solutions using the ICAO standards as their excuse. We have already seen the EU propose a central fingerprint registry; others may follow.

The current plans to store the biometrics on 'contact-less integrated circuits' also raises a number of concerns. This is likely to involve the use of radio-frequency identification (RFID) chips. RFID-tagged passports could be secretly read right through a wallet, pocket, backpack, or purse by anyone with the appropriate reader device, including marketers, identity thieves, pickpockets, oppressive governments, and others. The ICAO is promoting the adoption of this technology even as RFID chips are stirring deep concerns and controversy around the world. It would be premature to finalize a choice of technology without consideration of these issues. Use of these chips must be re-considered, assessed, and compared with alternative technologies that are less invasive.

National biometric databases and the retention of biometrics by third-parties can be avoided. The ICAO could have been wiser in its selection of technology, and more specific in its implementation. Biometrics can be implemented in such ways that they are prevented from being used for surreptitious surveillance or tracking. Biometrics can be stored locally on travel documents, and border checks can simply verify the link between the individual's live biometric and the biometric template stored on the actual document. Such two-way checks have been considered by the ICAO, but unfortunately are not part of the ICAO requirements. In addition, as EU privacy officials have written,

> biometric systems related to physical characteristics which do not leave traces (e.g. shape of the hand but not fingerprints) or biometrics systems related to physical characteristics which leave traces but do not rely on the memorisation of the data in the possession of someone other than the individual concerned (in other words, the data is not memorised in the control access device or in a central data base) create less risks for the protection for fundamental rights and freedoms of individuals.

Such care in the creation of the standards has not been demonstrated by ICAO so far. The ICAO must go back and reconsider its choices and conduct a review of all available technologies and their likely effects on privacy and civil liberties.

"States [can] protect the confidentiality and integrity of the . . . [biometric] data while severely controlling its availability or use."

Biometric Travel Documents Would Protect Americans

International Civil Aviation Organization

The International Civil Aviation Organization (ICAO) is the United Nations agency that works toward safe and sustainable development of civil aviation. In the following viewpoint it endorses the encoding of biometric identifiers—such as a person's fingerprints, iris scan, and photographs—into travel documents. Biometrics, it explains, have numerous applications in helping authorities verify passengers' identity. Face recognition is the preferred biometric method because, the ICAO avows, it is nonintrusive and uses information that is routinely disclosed to the general public. This viewpoint is excerpted from an ICAO technical report designed to aid states in their implementation of biometrics in travel documents.

"Biometrics Deployment of Machine Readable Travel Documents, Version 2.06," International Civil Aviation Organization, May 21, 2004, pp. 5, 8, 14, 17–19, 45. Reproduced by permission of ICAO.

As you read, consider the following questions:

1. How does the ICAO define biometrics?
2. Name three applications of biometrics, as set forth by the author.
3. In the ICAO's view, what are four benefits of using facial recognition to verify identity?

ICAO [International Civil Aviation Organization] New Technologies Working Group (NTWG) has, as a key tenet, been undertaking a program focusing on machine assisted identity confirmation of persons, both in terms of identification at the time of initial issue of travel documents, and in terms of verification for border control purposes.

At the core of this program is biometrics, being the way of uniquely encoding a particular physical characteristic of a person into a biometric-identifier (also known as a biometric template) that can be machine-verified to confirm the presenter's identity. In ultimate terms this could enable self-verification of an individual, and as a minimum it can provide assistance for verification personnel as to the potential the person presenting is an impostor.

NTWG has authored a number of Technical Reports, initially specifying race, fingerprint and iris (one or a combination thereof) as the biometrics to be used by States and subsequently resolving that face is the biometric most suited to the practicalities of travel document issuance, with fingerprint and/or iris available for choice by States for inclusion as complementary biometric technologies. Additional NTWG Technical Reports have specified a Logical Data Structure [LDS] in which to electronically encode the biometric in a travel document, and the use of PKI (Public Key Infrastructure) schemes to protect and authenticate the data so-encoded. . . .

What Are Biometrics?

"Biometrics" are the automated means of recognising a living person through the measurement of distinguishing physiological or behavioural traits. A "biometric template" is a machine-encoded representation of the trait created by a computer software algorithm, and enables comparisons (matches) to be performed to score the degree of confidence that separately recorded traits identify (or do not identify) the same person.

In the context of this Technical Report, the biometrics referred to are the physiological ones of

- facial recognition
- fingerprint
- iris

which were selected and endorsed by the 13th ICAO TAG/ MRTD [Technical Advisory Group on Machine Readable Travel Documents] in February 2002 in the original *NTWG Biometrics Selection Technical Report*.

Furthermore the purpose of this *Biometrics Deployment Technical Report* is to provide guidelines for States in the introduction and deployment of biometrics with respect to Machine Readable Travel Documents (MRTD) and their holders, border security and border control.

There are three (3) types of MRTD:

- A *passport* asserts the person is a citizen of the issuing State
- A *visa* asserts the State issuing the visa has granted the non-citizen the privilege of entering and remaining in the issuing State for a specified time and purpose
- *Other travel documents* are essentially special purpose identification/border-crossing cards issued to non-citizens.

In biometrics terminology:

- *"verify"* means to perform a *one-to-one* match between proffered biometric data obtained from the MRTD holder now, and a biometric template created when the holder enrolled in the system.

- *"identify"* means to perform a *one-to-many* search between proffered biometric data and a collection of templates representing all of the subjects who have enrolled in the system. . . .

Many Applications of Biometrics

The key application of a biometrics solution is the identity verification problem of physically tying an MRTD holder to the MRTD they are carrying.

There are several typical applications for biometrics during the enrolment process of applying for a passport or visa:

1. The applicant's biometric template(s) generated by the enrolment process can be searched against one or more biometric databases (identification) to determine whether the applicant is known to any of the corresponding systems (for example, holding a passport under a different identity, criminal record, holding a passport from another state).

2. When the applicant collects the passport or visa (or presents themselves for any step in the issuance process after the initial application is made and the biometric data is captured) their biometric data can be taken again and verified against the initially captured template.

3. The identities of the staff undertaking the enrolment can be verified to confirm they have the authority to perform their assigned tasks. This may include biometric authentication to initiate digital signature of audit logs of various steps in the issuance process, allowing biometrics to link the staff members to those actions for which they are responsible.

There are also several typical applications for biometrics at the border:

1. Each time travellers (i.e. MRTD holders) enter or exit a State, their identities can be verified against the images or templates created at the time their travel documents were issued. This will ensure that the holder of a document is the legitimate person to whom it was issued and will enhance the effectiveness of any Advance Passenger Information (API) system [which collects data on travellers before their arrival]. Ideally, the biometric template or templates should be stored on the travel document along with the image, so that travellers' identities can be verified in locations where access to the central database is unavailable or for jurisdictions where permanent centralized storage of biometric data is unacceptable.

2. Two-way check—The traveller's current captured biometric image data, and the biometric template from their travel document (or from a central database), can be matched to confirm that the travel document has not been altered.

3. Three-way check—The traveller's current biometric image data, the image from their travel document, and the image stored in a central database can be matched (via constructing biometric templates of each) to confirm that the travel document has not been altered. This technique matches the person, with their passport, with the database recording the data that was put in that passport at the time it was issued.

4. Four-way check—A fourth confirmatory check, albeit not an electronic one, is visually matching the results of the 3-way check with the digitised photograph on the Data Page of the traveller's passport.

The Berlin Resolution

By June 2002, it was clear to NTWG that a guideline was needed to assist States in prioritising their investigations [into biometric technologies]. Consequently at the June 2002 meeting of NTWG in Berlin, the following resolution was unanimously endorsed:

ICAO TAG-MRTD/NTWG RESOLUTION N001—Berlin, 28 June 2002

ICAO TAG-MRTD/NTWG endorses the use of face recognition as the globally interoperable biometric for machine assisted identity confirmation with machine readable travel documents.

ICAO TAG-MRTD/NTWG further recognizes that Member States may elect to use fingerprint and/or iris recognition as additional biometric technologies in support of machine assisted identity confirmation. *Endorsement:* Unanimous

In reaching this resolution, NTWG observed that for the majority of States the following advantages applied to face [recognition]:

- Facial photographs do not disclose information that the person does not routinely disclose to the general public

- The photograph (facial image) is already socially and culturally accepted internationally

- It is already collected and verified routinely as part of the MRTD application form process in order to produce a passport to ICAO Document 9303 standards

- The public are already aware of its capture and use for identity verification purposes

- It is non-intrusive—the user does not have to touch or interact with a physical device for a substantial time-frame to be enrolled

- It does not require new and costly enrolment procedures to be introduced

- Capture of it can be deployed relatively immediately and the opportunity to capture face retrospectively is also available

- Many States have a legacy database of facial images

captured as part of the digitised production of passport photographs which can be encoded into facial templates and verified against for identity comparison purposes

- It can be captured from an endorsed photograph, not requiring the person to be physically present

- It allows capture of children's biometrics without the children having to be present

- For watch lists, face (photograph) is generally the only biometric available for comparison

- It always acquires

- Human verification of the biometric against the photograph/person is relatively simple and a familiar process for border control authorities

At the Berlin Meeting, the NTWG unanimously supported its preference for the use of facial recognition as the globally interoperable biometric, noting that whilst it is recognized that research in this area is not yet complete, there is no evidence to suggest that facial recognition cannot be made to work in both the document issuance and border control environments. . . .

The New Orleans Resolution

The Berlin Resolution received wide publication and interest from various countries and groups in terms of the clarification it provided to enable Member States to plan their biometrics deployment strategy. However, it was also noted that some confusion and interpretation difficulties existed with this resolution.

Consequently at the March 2003 NTWG Conference in New Orleans, USA, a clarification resolution was proposed and accepted which builds on, and further clarifies, the strategy articulated by the Berlin resolution.

Key additional clarification provided by the New Orleans resolution includes:

- Digitally stored images will be used for global interoperability purposes, and these will be "on-board," i.e. electronically, stored in the travel document
- These images are to be standardized (the *NTWG Biometrics Deployment Technical Report* is the document that in the first instance defines the standards)
- High capacity Contactless IC media[1] is the electronic storage medium endorsed by NTWG as the capacity expansion technology for use with MRTDs in the deployment of biometrics. . . .

How Data Is Protected

The Contactless IC Chip needs to be protected against Logical Tampering. This means protection, encryption and authentication of the data. . . .

Data can be protected by various means including:

- Protection of data integrity by use of a cryptographic check sum (enabling detection of whether data has been changed while at the same time facilitating retrieval without any need for decrypting)—the recommended strategy since it has now been determined that LDS [Logical Data Structure] data such as . . . facial images are not to be encrypted—see the *LDS Technical Report* for further clarification
- Protection of data integrity by use of digital watermarking, whereby secret digital bits are dispersively buried into an image without affecting its visual quality—States may choose to use such techniques for their own image verification purposes, but the techniques

1. A Contactless Integrated Circuit is a data-carrying computer chip that can be read remotely.

should not be regarded as globally interoperable because of their proprietary nature
- Protection of data integrity by use of a unique chip serial number to protect against cloning of chips
- Protection of data privacy by using cryptographic methods of authentication and data encryption using secret keys (symmetric or asymmetric)
- Providing a public infrastructure for key generation and management i.e. PKI.[2]

Use of PKI enables States to protect the confidentiality and integrity of the LDS data while severely controlling its availability for use. Using data encryption requires that a common key . . . be distributed to all locations where the template will be decrypted. Encryption can inherently provide an integrity check of the data. . . .

Authentication establishes the validity of the document and guards against forgeries or alteration. Public Key Infrastructure can be used to uniquely authenticate the source of the MRTD, to ensure that the electronic data therein has not been altered, and to protect the privacy of the data.

2. PKI is an initiative supporting the use of digital signatures in travel documents to help verify their authenticity.

| *"The company had installed hidden cameras in its restrooms—some cameras pointing directly at the urinals."*

Employee Monitoring Violates Privacy

National Workrights Institute

According to the National Workrights Institute (NWI) in the viewpoint that follows, employers regularly videotape workers, listen to their phone calls, spy on their Internet usage and Web searches, check their hard drives, and read their personal e-mails. Overall, these acts are extremely invasive, laments the NWI. The group also protests that employees often do not know that they are being monitored, when they are being monitored, or what activities may be monitored. In the NWI's opinion, employers must be barred from committing these indefensible intrusions into the lives of their employees. National Workrights Institute is dedicated to protecting human rights in the workplace.

As you read, consider the following questions:

1. In the NWI's assertion, what is erasing the boundary between the home and the workplace?

"Privacy Under Siege: Electronic Monitoring in the Workplace," National Workrights Institute, 2004, pp. 2–5, 10, 17. Reproduced by permission.

2. What technology does the author call the most invasive of all?

3. When employees work from home, what personal information might their employers gain access to, according to the NWI?

Everyone in the office knew that Gail would change her clothes in her cubicle for the gym after the work day was done. When her employers installed a hidden camera to monitor the person in the neighboring cubicle's suspected illegal activities, her daily ritual was captured on film. The first few times could have been labeled as mistakes, but the filming of Gail changing her clothes over a five month period was inexcusable.

[—Gail Nelson v. Salem State College]

Electronic monitoring is a rapidly growing phenomenon in American businesses. Introduced in the early twentieth century for such limited uses as timing breaks and measuring hand-eye movements, systematic electronic monitoring has since grown into the very fabric of American business practice. As technologies become more powerful and easy and inexpensive to install and maintain, the rates of electronic monitoring in this country have skyrocketed. In 1999 the percentage of employers who electronically monitor their workers was 67%. Just two years later, in the year 2001 this number had increased to 78%. By 2003, 92% of employers were conducting some form of workplace monitoring. This rapid growth in monitoring has virtually destroyed any sense of privacy as we know it in the American workplace. Employers now conduct video surveillance, listen in on employee telephone calls, review employee computer use such as e-mail and the Internet and monitor their every move using GPS [Global Positioning System]. But as legitimate work product is being monitored, so are the personal habits and lives of employees. As technology has proliferated in the workplace, it has become ever more penetrating and intrusive. And yet there are few, if any, legal protections for employees. There has been no attempt to balance employer demands with legitimate employee privacy concerns. Collection and use of personal information is a rampant byproduct of workplace monitoring and threatens the very freedoms that we cherish as Americans. Legislation is necessary to govern the practice of electronic monitoring in the workplace, protect employee privacy and return a sense of fundamental fairness and dignity to the American workplace.

Personal Communications in the Workplace

While employers generally initiate electronic monitoring in response to legitimate business concerns, the results have been devastating to employee privacy. Virtually everything we do and say at work can be, and is, monitored by our employers. Our employers watch us on video cameras, read our e-mails, listen to our voice mail, review documents on our hard drives, and check every web site we visit.

This would be bad enough if it involved only work related behavior and communication, but it doesn't. The advent of cell phones, pagers, and home computers is rapidly erasing the traditional wall between the home and the workplace. People now regularly receive communications from their employer at home. Maggie Jackson, former workplace correspondent for the Associated Press, estimates that the average professional or managerial employee now receives over 20 electronic messages from work every week. This new flexibility also means that personal communication increasingly occurs in the workplace. An employee who spent much of the weekend on a cell phone with her boss will not (and should not) consider it inappropriate to make a personal call from the office.

This means that employer monitoring systems frequently record personal communications. Often, this communication is not sensitive. But sometimes the messages are very personal. An employee who sends their spouse a romantic e-mail while eating lunch at his or her desk can find that their love letter has been read by their boss. Or a note to a psychiatrist stored in an employee's hard drive is disclosed.

Internet and Video Monitoring

Internet monitoring can be extremely invasive. People today turn to the Internet as their primary source of information, including sensitive subjects they would be uncomfortable communicating about on their office telephone or e-mail. In part, this is because of the efficiency of Internet research. Even an untrained person can find information on the web in minutes that would have taken hours or even days to find by traditional means (if they could find it at all). People also turn to the Internet for information because they can do so anonymously.

The result is that people turn to the Internet for information and help about the most sensitive subjects imaginable. Women who are victims of domestic abuse turn to the Internet for information about shelters and other forms of help. People also turn to the Web for information and help with drug and alcohol problems, financial difficulties, marital problems, and medical issues. Monitoring Web access gives an employer a picture window into employees' most sensitive personal problems.

Most invasive of all is video monitoring. Some cameras are appropriate. Security cameras in stairwells and parking garages make us all safer without intruding on privacy. But employers often install cameras in areas that are completely indefensible. Many employers have installed hidden video cameras in locker rooms and bathrooms, sometimes inside the stalls. No one should be subjected to sexual voyeurism on the job.

Improper Methods

Such problems are made worse by the manner in which monitoring is often conducted. Most employers make no effort to avoid monitoring personal communications. The majority of

Ted Rall. © 2001 distributed by Universal Press Syndicate. Reproduced by permission.

employers install systems that make no distinction between business and personal messages, even when more discriminating systems are available.

In addition to official monitoring, IT [information technology] employees often monitor their fellow employees for personal reasons. Most employers give such employees carte blanche access to employee communications. While it is possible to set up technical barriers to ensure that monitoring is confined to official programs, few employers use them. Many employers do not even have policies directing IT employees to restrict their monitoring to official programs. Even employers with such policies rarely have procedures to enforce them. As a result, employees involved in monitoring often read the messages of fellow employees for their own amusement.

The final indignity is that employees don't even know when they are being watched. While a majority of employers provide employees what is described as notice, still many do not and the information currently provided is generally useless. The standard employer notice states only that the company reserves the right to monitor anything at any time. Employees do not know whether it is their e-mail, voice mail, Web access, or hard drive that is monitored. They do not know whether the monitoring is continuous, random, or as needed. They do not even know whether they are being monitored at all. Such notice is almost worse than no notice at all.

Special Problems for Telecommuters

As bad as the situation is today, it is likely to be far worse in the future. Many people today do work for their employer on their home computers. The most direct example of this is telecommuting. Approximately 20 million employees and independent contractors now work at home at least one day per month, and this number is growing rapidly. Millions more have linked their home computer to their office network so they can work from home informally on evenings and weekends.

When this occurs, people's home computers are subject to monitoring by their employer. Workplace computer monitoring systems monitor the entire network, including a home computer that is temporarily part of the network. This means that personal communications in our home computers will be revealed to our employers. Personal e-mail sent from or received by our home computers will be disclosed to our employers, along with personal letters, financial records, and any other personal information in our home computers. Not only is this possible, it is highly likely. When asked if they would be interested in having personal information from employees' home computers, corporate attorneys responded positively.

Employers generally conduct electronic monitoring in order to increase productivity. It is far from clear, however, that monitoring achieves this goal. In fact, too much monitoring can actually decrease productivity by increasing employee stress and decreasing morale. . . .

Stories of Workplace Monitoring Across America

At a Neiman-Marcus Store in Fashion Island Newport Beach [California], Kelly Pendleton, a two-time "employee of the year" discovered a hidden camera in the ceiling of the changing room used by female employees that was being monitored by male colleagues.

Employees of Consolidated Freightways were horrified to find that the company had installed hidden cameras in its restrooms—some cameras pointing directly at the urinals. Over a thousand hours of video records were made covering thousands of employees. "The guys were really shaken, and some of the women went home crying," says Joe Quilty, the dockworker who discovered the hidden cameras.

An AT&T employee received a formal reprimand for using the company e-mail system to send a love note to his wife, also an AT&T employee. . . .

The explosion of workplace surveillance in recent years has stripped Americans of virtually all their privacy on the job. Nearly 80% of employers now use electronic surveillance. Soon it will be universal.

"Anyone who holds privacy dear to their heart should consider separating business from pleasure."

Employee Monitoring Does Not Violate Privacy

Kevin Beaver

Employee surveillance helps companies increase employee productivity, shield workers from offensive content, and protect themselves from lawsuits, explains Kevin Beaver in the following viewpoint. He stresses that employers should notify workers that their e-mails and Internet surfing may be reviewed by management and make clear what the consequences of inappropriate actions will be. Done in this way, there is nothing objectionable about monitoring, Beaver contends. Ultimately, employers have a right to decide how their computers and other property can be used, he argues. Kevin Beaver founded the information security consulting firm Principle Logic, LLC.

As you read, consider the following questions:

1. What point does the author make about fax machines and copiers?

Kevin Beaver, "Where Do You Draw the Line on Employee Monitoring?," SearchSecurity.com, October 17, 2002. Reproduced by permission.

2. According to Beaver, what makes for an effective monitoring system?

3. What is the author's view on zero tolerance?

Over the past few years, the employee monitoring waters have grown very murky. There are court cases that argue both sides of the story. Some see employee monitoring as a general best practice; others see it as an invasion of employee privacy and a highly charged issue of which they want to steer clear. Regardless of anyone's stance, the studies are out there that show that companies are losing major bucks, time and resources on non-business-based computer usage.

Not for Personal Use

Before the Internet era, monitoring computer usage was hardly an issue. Now, employees have such easy access to things like e-mail, instant messaging and Internet shopping that everything has changed. Management must understand that the idea of monitoring is new to most people and that their employees won't assume it is policy unless they are told so. I'm amazed that some managers are surprised when employees express their displeasure about lack of privacy in the workplace. Those are usually the same managers who didn't set employee expectations in the first place. The least management can do is to let their employees know what their acceptable usage policies are.

Don't worry. I'm not letting employees off the hook so easily. For a long time, it has been a policy at most companies that equipment such as the fax machine and copiers are not there for personal use. There should be some level of assumption on the employees' part that the same is true for company owned computers as well. They should expect that their privacy is not guaranteed when they utilize company equipment, and they most certainly shouldn't be offended when they know they are subject to being monitored. Employees are not hired to tend to personal Internet and e-mail matters—they are hired to perform certain tasks in exchange for compensation. Can they truly blame management for having a vested interest in what they do on company time and with company equipment?

Effective Monitoring

As a manager, there are human resources, legal and IT [information technology] issues related to employee monitoring that you must consider. Some of these include: employee productivity; protecting employees against offensive content; protecting the business (and shareholders) from sexual harassment, defamation and illegal activity lawsuits; employee morale; policy enforcement; and network bandwidth consumption. An effective employee-monitoring system is one that employees understand and buy in to, runs quietly in the background without getting in the way of employee productivity, can be easily referred to when needed and does not place any unnecessary time or resource burdens on the IT department.

If you are a manager responsible for monitoring employees, you should remember to document what type of monitoring is being done, make your employees aware of it, and use technology to help enforce it. Unless you want to count on your gut feeling that something is wrong, you'll have to rely on certain technologies like content filtering and other monitoring applications to enforce your acceptable usage policies. All that being said, employee monitoring is not an IT issue, so don't let technology get in the way. Technology only comes into play when it's time to enforce the policies that have already been established.

Considering Employee Morale

Like other areas where zero tolerance is instituted, it won't work with employee monitoring, either. You have to ask yourself, if Stan in accounting or Bob in the mailroom check their

Many Benefits of Employee Monitoring

Monitoring is an effective deterrent and detection technique. . . . One important component of prevention is establishing the business purposes of monitoring, which may include the following:

- Preventing misuse of resources. Companies can discourage unproductive personal activities such as online shopping or web surfing on company time. Monitoring employee performance is one way to reduce unnecessary network traffic and reduce the consumption of network bandwidth.

- Promoting adherence to policies. Online surveillance is one means of verifying employee observance of company networking policies.

- Preventing lawsuits. Firms can be held liable for discrimination or employee harassment in the workplace. Organizations can also be involved in infringement suits through employees that distribute copyrighted material over corporate networks.

- Safeguarding records. Federal legislation requires organizations to protect personal information. . . .

- Safeguarding company assets. The protection of intellectual property, trade secrets, and business strategies is a major concern. The case of information transmission and storage makes it imperative to monitor employee actions as part of a broader policy.

Robin L. Wakefield, CPA Journal, *July 2004.*

e-mail or surf the Web during their lunch break or other down time—is that really going to affect your bottom line?

An employee-monitoring program has got to be realistic. It shouldn't be about power or curiosity but rather about productivity and protecting the business' best interests.

When employee monitoring comes into play, there is always employee morale to consider. I believe that you can strike a balance between employee monitoring and employee job satisfaction. Having trouble getting buy-in from your current employees? Lead by example to help influence your organization's culture. Of course, some people aren't going to be happy—change breeds contempt. It's much easier to integrate employee monitoring as early on as possible in the life of your company because it's only human for employees to resist giving up their "privacy" once they've had it for a while. Establish trust, and let your employees do their jobs with the knowledge that if they do something that you define as unacceptable, there will be consequences. If your acceptable usage policies state "this is the way we do it here at XYZ Company," then your employees can go into this with their eyes wide open. If you're up front about it and make it clear what is being monitored and what your business reasons are for doing it, your employees will buy into it. Do they have a choice?

If acceptable usage policies and employee awareness programs are implemented properly by management, employees will know what to expect. I believe that anyone who holds privacy dear to their heart should consider separating business from pleasure. I'm a strong believer and supporter of personal freedoms, but I also think that employers should have the right to decide how their own property is used. Until the courts sort all of this out, it is up to each company to decide where to draw the line.

Periodical Bibliography

Clyde Wayne Crews Jr.	"Monitoring Biometric Technologies in a Free Society," *USA Today (Magazine)*, July 2003.
European Civil Aviation Conference	"Biometrics," presented to the ICAO summit, Cairo, Egypt, March 22–April 2, 2004. www.i-cao.int.
Terry Jones	"It's the Internet, Stupid," *St. Louis Journalism Review*, October 2003.
Ted Koppel	"Take My Privacy, Please!" *New York Times*, June 13, 2005.
Etelka Lehoczky	"Watch Yourself—You Might Be Monitored," *Boston Globe*, October 10, 2004.
Tom Ridge	"Remarks at the Center for Strategic and International Studies," Washington, DC, January 12, 2005. www.dhs.gov.
Eugene Volokh	"Big Brother Is Watching—Be Grateful!" *Wall Street Journal*, March 26, 2002.
Robin L. Wakefield	"Employee Monitoring and Surveillance—The Growing Trend," *CPA Journal*, July 2004.
Dick Zunkel	"The Other Side of Privacy: Protecting Information with Biometrics," *Security Technology & Design*, June 2005.

OPPOSING
VIEWPOINTS®
SERIES

CHAPTER 3

Is Medical Privacy Adequately Protected?

Chapter Preface

Approximately 20 percent of U.S. abortions are performed on teenagers. To ensure that minors consult their parents before obtaining the procedure, forty-four states have laws on the books requiring parental notification or consent. In some states youths can bypass this requirement by obtaining a judicial waiver. Proponents of these laws contend that minors are less mature than adults and need the guidance of their parents, especially in making health care decisions such as whether or not to have an abortion. Children's rights advocates counter, however, that the laws violate a girl's right to keep her health status and medical procedures confidential. They cite the Hippocratic Oath, which doctors have an ethical duty to uphold: "Whatsoever things I see or hear concerning the life of men, in my attentance on the sick or even apart therefrom, which ought not be noised abroad, I will keep silence thereon, counting such things to be as sacred secrets." Citizens who wish for complete protection of the "sacred secrets" of their health sometimes clash with others who feel that special situations justify violating patients' privacy.

Nearly 80 percent of Americans surveyed in 2000 felt it was "very important" that their medical records be kept confidential. Medical records often list patients' name, Social Security number, birth date, and current maladies as well as their history of medical ailments, treatments, and psychiatric care. However, some analysts argue that youths' right to privacy is outweighed by their parents' need to be informed of their health. Supporters of parental notification laws offer the example of twelve-year-old Crystal Lane. Her mother did not know that Rosa Hartford's eighteen-year-old son had impregnated her. Because Pennsylvania law requires parental consent before a minor may have an abortion, Hartford took Lane to New York, a state that had no such laws, where she underwent an abortion. Critics believe that Hartford had no right to help

Lane make such a decision without involving the girl's parents. Abortion doctor Bruce A. Lucero points out, "Parents are usually the ones who can best help their teen-ager consider her options. And whatever the girl's decision, parents can provide the necessary emotional support."

Most everyone agrees that it would be ideal if every adolescent could discuss intimate matters such as sex and pregnancy with her parents. However, some people maintain that attempting to force such communication by way of parental consent or notification laws could jeopardize youths' welfare. These commentators assert that a teen who hides her pregnancy from her parents does so for compelling reasons. For example, she may have abusive or neglectful parents who would harm or abandon her upon learning of her sexual activity. Moreover, although girls may obtain a court waiver to bypass parental notification, rights advocates note that the judicial process may be time-consuming and intimidating to them. Abortion rights supporter Diana Philip warns, "When a minor seeks legal relief through the courts, her abortion procedure is delayed, increasing the costs, and at times, the risk of complications in terminating a pregnancy at a more progressed stage."

Clearly both sides make strong points for and against preserving the medical privacy of adolescents who wish to obtain an abortion. In the following chapter authors continue the debate by discussing the circumstances, if any, under which medical privacy should be compromised. Because Americans value medical confidentiality so highly, the issue is likely to remain contentious well into the future.

> "The rule protects the confidentiality of
> Americans' medical records without
> creating new barriers to receiving
> quality health care."

Federal Law Protects Patients' Privacy

U.S. Department of Health and Human Services

The U.S. Department of Health and Human Services (HHS) is the governmental agency responsible for protecting the health of Americans. According to HHS in the following viewpoint, a federal law was amended in April 2003 to better safeguard Americans' medical privacy. Health care providers, hospitals, and insurers covered by the legislation now are required to inform patients of their privacy rights, HHS states. Additionally, the agency claims, the law provides instructions for the use and release of patients' health information, requires authorization before patients' information can be used for nonroutine purposes such as marketing, generally allows patients to inquire about nonroutine disclosures of their records, and offers an avenue of recourse for patients if their medical privacy is violated.

U.S. Department of Health and Human Services, "HHS Issues First Major Protections for Patient Privacy," August 9, 2002. www.hhs.gov.

As you read, consider the following questions:

1. What does the privacy rule say regarding the mailing of marketing materials to patients?
2. What example does HHS give of an unintended consequence of HIPAA that would have hindered patients' access to quality health care?
3. According to HHS, what is the Office for Civil Rights doing to help people prepare for the privacy rule changes?

HHS [U.S. Department of Health and Human Services] Secretary Tommy G. Thompson today [August 9, 2002] issued the first-ever comprehensive federal regulation[1] that gives patients sweeping protections over the privacy of their medical records. The final regulation, which takes effect April 14, 2003, will ensure strong privacy protections without interfering with Americans' access to quality health care.

The federal privacy regulation empowers patients by guaranteeing them access to their medical records, giving them more control over how their protected health information is used and disclosed, and providing a clear avenue of recourse if their medical privacy is compromised. The rule will protect medical records and other personal health information maintained by certain health care providers, hospitals, health plans, health insurers and health care clearinghouses.

"Patients now will have a strong foundation of federal protections for the personal medical information that they share with their doctors, hospitals and others who provide their care and help pay for it," Secretary Thompson said. "The rule protects the confidentiality of Americans' medical records without creating new barriers to receiving quality health care.

---

1. The regulation comes in the form of amendments to the Health Insurance Portability and Accountability Act of 1996 (HIPAA).

It strikes a common sense balance by providing consumers with personal privacy protections and access to high quality care."

Provisions

Under the privacy rule:

- Patients must give specific authorization before entities covered by this regulation could use or disclose protected information in most non-routine circumstances—such as releasing information to an employer or for use in marketing activities. Doctors, health plans and other covered entities would be required to follow the rule's standards for the use and disclosure of personal health information.

- Covered entities generally will need to provide patients with written notice of their privacy practices and patients' privacy rights. The notice will contain information that could be useful to patients choosing a health plan, doctor or other provider. Patients would generally be asked to sign or otherwise acknowledge receipt of the privacy notice from direct treatment providers.

- Pharmacies, health plans and other covered entities must first obtain an individual's specific authorization before sending them marketing materials. At the same time, the rule permits doctors and other covered entities to communicate freely with patients about treatment options and other health-related information, including disease-management programs.

- Specifically, improvements to the final rule strengthen the marketing language to make clear that covered entities cannot use business associate agreements to circumvent the rule's marketing prohibition. The improvement explicitly prohibits pharmacies or other covered entities from selling personal medical information to a business that wants to market its products or services under a business associate agreement.

- Patients generally will be able to access their personal medical records and request changes to correct any errors. In addition, patients generally could request an accounting of non-routine uses and disclosures of their health information.

Taking the Public's Needs into Consideration

HHS issued privacy regulations in December 2000 but had to make changes to address the serious unintended consequences of the rule that would have interfered with patients' access to quality care. For example, patients would have been required to visit a pharmacy in person to sign paperwork before a pharmacist could review protected health information in order to fill their prescriptions. Similar barriers would have arisen when a patient is referred to a specialist and in other situations.

"We took great care to make sure we weren't creating greater hardships or more health care bureaucracy for patients as they seek to get prompt and effective care," Secretary Thompson said. "The prior regulation, while well-intentioned, would have forced sick or injured patients to run all around town getting signatures before they could get care or medicine. This regulation gives patients the power to protect their privacy and still get efficient health care."

HHS received more than 11,000 public comments on the proposed modifications issued in March 2002 and today is adopting final changes. The final version, which will be published in the Aug. 14th [2002] Federal Register, includes some key revisions to address public concerns. The rule will be available online today at www.hhs.gov/ocr/hipaa/.

A Government Official Explains How the HIPAA Modifications Affect Patients' Privacy

The Privacy Rule modifications removed the requirement that providers must obtain prior consent to use or disclose a patient's health information for treatment, payment or health care operations purposes. While obtaining such consent is optional, this change assured that providers would have ready access to health information about their patients, and could readily share that information for treatment, for payment, and for health care operations so that timely access to quality health care would not be unduly impeded. At the same time, we strengthened the notice requirement by requiring direct treatment providers to make a good faith effort to obtain the patient's written acknowledgment that they received the notice. This ensures that a patient has the opportunity to consider the provider's privacy practices, both to be better informed of how their information may or may not be disclosed, and to be informed of their rights—which had been a primary goal of the consent requirement. Notably, the Privacy Rule retained the protections that give patients the right to decide whether to authorize uses or disclosures of their information for marketing purposes, or to employers. . . .

The Privacy Rule, as modified, both protects patient information, but avoids imposing unnecessary impediments to quality health care.

Richard Campanelli, statement before the U.S. Senate Special Committee on Aging, Washington, D.C., September 23, 2003.

Preparation for the Privacy Rule

HHS' privacy regulation is designed to enhance the protections afforded by many existing state laws. Stronger state laws and other federal laws continue to apply, so the federal regulation provides a national base of privacy protections. The standards for covered entities apply whether its patients are privately insured, uninsured or covered under public programs such as Medicare or Medicaid.

Most covered entities have until April 14, 2003, to comply with the patient privacy rule; under the law, certain small health plans have until April 14, 2004, to comply.

To help people prepare for and meet the rule's requirements, HHS' Office for Civil Rights (OCR) will continue to conduct outreach and education targeted to health plans, health care providers, consumers and others affected by the privacy regulation.

These efforts include developing appropriate technical assistance materials, which may include fact sheets, handbooks and other materials, as well as responding to frequently asked questions. HHS also will hold national educational conferences in the fall [2002] to address issues related to key parts of the privacy regulation. Technical assistance materials will be posted on OCR's privacy rule website at www.hhs.gov/ocr/hipaa/.

"We are working to do our part to educate the health care industry and the public about these rights and protections in advance of the April 2003 compliance date required under the law," OCR director Richard M. Campanelli said. "We believe the improvements in this final rule will be helpful to both health care providers and the public. Our goal is to ensure patients enjoy their full federal privacy rights and protections by helping covered entities follow the rule."

In 1996, Congress recognized the need for national patient privacy standards and, as part of the Health Insurance Portability and Accountability Act of 1996 (HIPAA), set a three-year deadline for it to enact such protections. HIPAA also required that, if Congress did not meet this deadline, HHS was to adopt health information privacy protections via regulation based upon certain specific parameters included in HIPAA. Congress did not enact health privacy legislation.

HHS proposed federal privacy standards in 1999 and, after reviewing and considering more than 52,000 public comments on them, published final standards in December 2000. In March 2001, Secretary Thompson requested additional public input and received more than 11,000 comments, which helped to shape the improvements proposed in March 2002. Today's final improvements reflect public comments received on that proposal.

> "The Hippocratic Oath—the founda-
> tion of medical ethics and the most
> important of all patients' rights—has
> been rescinded by federal decree."

Federal Law Violates Patients' Privacy

Barry K. Herman and Deborah C. Peel

In 2003 the federal government modified the Health Insurance Portability and Accountability Act of 1996 (HIPAA). The authors of the following viewpoint, psychiatrists Barry K. Herman and Deborah C. Peel, are alarmed about the effects the change may have on medical privacy. Under the amended HIPAA, they contend, a patient's lifetime medical information can be disclosed without consent or notice to private corporations and government entities and their business associates. Herman and Peel predict that patients who fear that their privacy will be breached will avoid seeing doctors, will withhold sensitive information from their medical providers, or will lie about their health, compromising their own health care.

Barry K. Herman and Deborah C. Peel, "HIPAA's Real Effect: The End of Medical Privacy; a New Dilemma for Physician Executives," *Physician Executive*, vol. 30, January/February 2004, pp. 34–38. Reproduced by permission.

141

As you read, consider the following questions:

1. What entities are covered under HIPAA, as stated by Herman and Peel?

2. In the authors' contention, what was the problem with the three privacy notices examined by a federal district court?

3. What right did the Supreme Court affirm in *Jaffee v. Redmond*, according to Herman and Peel?

Every American's entire medical record became an open book on April 14, 2003, the final effective date for compliance with the amendments to the Health Insurance Portability and Accountability Act of 1996 (HIPAA) privacy rule. On that day, every American lost the right to consent to the release of his/her medical records, as a matter of federal law and policy.

The administration did not inform the nation when it eliminated every individual's right to consent to the release of his/her medical records in a few sentences buried deep within the amendments to the privacy rule.

The lack of clear notice also contributed to the media's and the public's focus on compliance, instead of on the loss of the right to consent. The far-reaching effects of the current regulations have yet to be appreciated by the public at large, by the media or by physicians.

No Consent, Notice, or Recourse

The amendments to the HIPAA privacy rule grant breathtakingly broad and unprecedented powers to both private corporations and government entities to collect and amass the individual medical data of every person in the United States.

The new doctrine of federal regulatory permission gives over 600,000 "covered entities" and their innumerable business associates the right to access every American's cradle-to-grave medical records without consent, without notice and without recourse.

Even if treatment is paid for out-of-pocket or an individual never has another contact with the health care system, his or her personal health information may now be accessed for purposes of "health care operations."

In announcing the amendment to the privacy rule, the U.S. Health and Human Services Department (HHS) stated that "the consent provisions in 164.506 are replaced with a new provision at 164.506(a) that provides regulatory permission for covered entities to use or disclose protected health information for treatment, payment, and health care operations."

In a briefing to congressional staff on August 19, 2002. Jim Pyles, a medical privacy expert, wrote that: "The privacy rule applies to covered entities and their business associates."

Covered entities are health plans (such as HMOs and Medicare Part A and B), health care clearinghouses (entities that process health information), and health care providers (any person or entity who furnishes, bills or is paid for health care). Business associates are a broad range of entities and individuals that provide services to or for covered entities.

HHS estimated that the privacy rule affects "over 600,000 entities and virtually every American." The health information that can be covered by the privacy rule is virtually any identifiable health information relating to the "past, present, or future physical or mental condition of an individual."

The amendments to the privacy rule permit these covered entities and business associates to use and disclose identifiable health information for three broad purposes—treatment, payment and health care operations.

Many of these purposes, particularly health care operations activities are related to the business operations of covered entities rather than the need to provide health care to an individual. They include, for example, business planning and development, and business management and general administrative services.

Jim Borgman, "Please sign here to indicate . . .," 2003. © King Features Syndicate. Reproduced by permission.

The definitions of treatment, payment and health care operations are so broad that they encompass most of the uses and disclosures of health information.

Under the amendments, hundreds of thousands of entities and individuals nationwide will be able to use and disclose identifiable health information without the patient's consent or permission so long as they contend that they need it for a purpose related to treatment, payment and health care operations.

It is unlikely that any identifiable health information would be immune from use and disclosure without the patient's consent under this standard.

Destructive Consequences

The elimination of the right to medical privacy in the HIPAA regulations poses profound ethical and legal dilemmas for physician executives.

If the amendments to HIPAA are allowed to stand, the loss of consent will radically alter the physician-patient relationship and destroy the trust that patients must feel in order to share sensitive medical information.

If there is one thing in the over 1,500 pages of dense federal regulations that every patient will come to understand, it is the loss of the right of consent—that is, the right to control the use and disclosure of one's own individual health information.

When patients realize neither they nor their treating physicians have the right to stop the flow of sensitive medical information out of doctor's offices and other treatment sites, they will vote with their feet. They will avoid medical care for as long as possible, they will omit sensitive information or they will provide false information to try to protect themselves.

If the loss of medical privacy stands, it may also create a "black market" of completely private medical care for those few individuals who can afford it.

And finally, if this new federal doctrine eliminating the right to consent is not reversed, currently existing stronger medical privacy laws in every state will fall as industries that profit from access to identifiable medical information pressure each state legislature to eliminate the right of consent. Pressure to weaken existing privacy laws is already underway in Texas and Oregon.

In effect, the Hippocratic Oath—the foundation of medical ethics and the most important of all patients' rights—has been rescinded by federal decree.

Inadequate Privacy Notices

The HIPAA regulations provide only a floor for patient privacy, not a ceiling. Most HIPAA attorneys have not advised clients, including institutions, health plans, hospitals, group and solo practice physicians, and other covered entities of the

extent of their legal and ethical obligations under the HIPAA privacy rules.

They have neglected to inform clients that they are required to give patients notice about how to utilize greater medical privacy protections contained in state laws.

Furthermore, HIPAA specifies that physicians and health professionals should continue to use and follow the long-standing professional codes of ethics for their field or specialty and should develop privacy policies and notices in accordance with these traditional ethical principles.

Sample privacy notices were included as part of the basis for a lawsuit filed against HHS on April 10, 2003, in federal district court in Philadelphia, Pa. The lawsuit aims to overturn the amendments to HIPAA, which eliminate the right to consent. (See *Citizens for Health v. Tommy G. Thompson, Secretary: US Dept of HHS*)

As noted in the lawsuit, a review of three sample privacy notices found that patients were not being advised of the existence of more stringent state and common laws governing medical privacy that override the lesser federal protections in the HIPAA floor.

In each case, the privacy notices did not inform patients about how to exercise their rights to prevent access to their medical records under state statutory and common law. . . .

Ethical Questions

Physician executives are at the nexus of conflicting duties— duties to patients and duties to their employers or parent institutions. The amendments to HIPAA that eliminate the right of consent will add new and uncomfortable ethical and legal burdens.

Corporate legal and fiduciary responsibilities are clearly to shareholders. Physicians' codes of ethics require physicians to put the needs of patients first.

Physician executives can provide ethical and legal guidance to corporations and institutions that view the right of consent as a barrier to treatment or research and do not know the state and common laws and ethical principles that physicians must uphold.

The perspective that physicians provide to employers and institutions can make the case for protecting privacy crystal clear. Without trust, patients will avoid any treatment or tests that have the potential for discrimination, job loss, or shame and embarrassment.

Without trust, they will distort or omit critical information. Then, not only will the quality and efficacy of their care be compromised, but also the accuracy of information in health databases will be corrupted and unreliable.

In the area of mental health, psychiatrists know from direct experience how far many patients and parents will go to protect their children or their jobs, or to hide or omit information to keep others from knowing intimate personal or family information. Patients would conceal crucial medical information if they knew it would be available on the Internet.

In fact, the U.S. Supreme Court recognized that effective psychotherapy cannot exist without an absolute guarantee of privacy.

In *Jaffee v. Redmond* (1996), justices rejected any balancing test to weigh the needs of private individuals or entities against the right of patients to have privacy. The court noted that it was in the best interests of the nation to have effective psychotherapy available for citizens, so they affirmed the absolute right to privacy of the communications between patient and psychotherapist in recognizing a therapist-patient privilege. . . .

Eternal Vigilance Is Needed

Physician executives can advocate with employers, institutions, Congress and government agencies to restore the right to consent and enact other privacy measures. The public strongly supports the right to the privacy of the most sensitive information that exists about them—their medical records.

No single approach to medical privacy can preserve such crucial rights. When the privacy rights of individuals are pitted against corporations and governmental agencies that want unfettered access to the most valuable personal information that exists, eternal vigilance is the only effective response.

"Genetic data poses significant privacy issues because it can serve as an identifier and can also convey sensitive personal information about the individual and his or her family."

Law Enforcement DNA Databanks Threaten Medical Privacy

Electronic Privacy Information Center

In order to prevent and solve crimes, the FBI collects and stores some people's DNA—genetic information that is unique to every individual—in computer databases. In the viewpoint that follows, the Electronic Privacy Information Center (EPIC) maintains that this cataloging of DNA has grave implications for privacy rights. For one thing, the organization claims, DNA information should be protected more than fingerprints are because DNA serves as an identifier and can reveal telling details about people's—and their families'—traits and diseases. Another of EPIC's concerns is that DNA databanks may be breached, resulting in highly sensitive data being released. The group also al-

"Genetic Privacy," Electronic Privacy Information Center, July 23, 2004, pp. 3–7. www.epic.org. Reproduced by permission.

leges that the forced collection of criminal suspects' DNA without a search warrant, which occurs in most U.S. jurisdictions, is a privacy violation. EPIC is a public interest research center focused on protecting privacy and other civil liberties.

As you read, consider the following questions:

1. What comprises DNA databanks, as stated by EPIC?
2. In EPIC's opinion, what is worrisome about science's ability to extract more personal information from less material?
3. In discussing the security of DNA databanks, what does EPIC say creates several points at which privacy can be violated?

Genetic information about any organism is contained in the organism's DNA (deoxyribonucleic acid) molecules. DNA is contained in all of the organism's cells except mature red blood cells. Every cell has two pairs of chromosomes, composed of DNA, except gamete cells (sperm and egg), which have only one set. DNA provides exact instructions for the creation and functioning of the organism. DNA molecules of all organisms contain the same basic physical and chemical components, arranged in different sequences. The *genome* is an organism's complete set of DNA.

DNA and DNA Databanks

The current estimate is that humans have between 32,000 and 35,000 genes. About 99.9 percent of the genome is the same in all humans. The arrangement of the remaining components is unique to most individuals. Only identical twins (or triplets, etc.) have identical DNA. Variations in DNA influence how individuals respond to disease, environmental factors such as bacteria, viruses, toxins, chemicals, and to drugs and other therapies. The interaction between genes and environmental factors is not well understood at this time and is the subject of intensive research.

Any properly stored tissue sample can be the source of DNA. *Handbook of Human Tissue Sources*, published by RAND, estimated that in 1999 there were more than 307 million tissue specimens stored in the United States, and that the number was growing by 20 million per year. These specimens are collected and stored for research, medical treatment, law enforcement, military identification, blood and tissue banking, fertility treatments and, increasingly, commercial purposes. However, not all tissue collections can be classified as DNA databanks. DNA databanks are composed of a set of tissue specimens, digital DNA profiles, stored in a computer database, and some form of linking between each specimen and the DNA profile derived from it. DNA databanks used in medical and research applications also include links to medical records and family history of individuals whose DNA is stored. Blood and tissue specimens can be preserved indefinitely, and DNA from these specimens can be tested multiple times.

Highly Sensitive Information

Genetic data poses significant privacy issues because it can serve as an identifier and can also convey sensitive personal information about the individual and his or her family. As genetic science develops, genetic information provides a growing amount of information about diseases, traits, and predispositions. At the same time, smaller and smaller tissue samples are required for testing. In some cases tests can be performed with as little as the root of a single hair or saliva left on a glass from which an individual drank. The ability to derive more information from less and less material creates increasing challenges to privacy because it permits analysis of tiny traces that all humans leave behind unconsciously, such as cells left on computer keys or saliva left on a drinking glass.

The ability of genetic information to provide both identification and sensitive information related to health and other predisposition has led to a lively debate about appropriate privacy protections. Proponents of "genetic exceptionalism" claim that genetic information deserves explicit and stricter protection under the law. They base their argument on the special qualities of genetic material:

- Ubiquity, i.e., the ability to derive genetic profiles from small physical traces and the longevity of material from which genetic profiles can be derived

- Ability to reveal information not just about the individual but also about the individual's family

- Predictive nature that can point to someone's future health and traits

Opponents of "genetic exceptionalism" take the position that genetic information is much like other personal information and should be protected in the same way. They point to the fact that "genetic information" is difficult to define because it includes information like family medical history, which has been collected and used by doctors long before the sequencing of the genome. Therefore, they emphasize the importance of context in which genetic information is obtained and used. For example, if genetic information is obtained as part of health care research or treatment, it should be subject to the same privacy and anti-discrimination protections as all other health information.

At present there is no specific protection for DNA information at the federal level in the United States. . . .

The use of DNA in identification is growing. DNA 'fingerprinting' is a process in which a laboratory creates a profile of specific agreed-upon segments ('loci') of the DNA molecule. In order to identify a particular individual, the laboratory compares the profile produced from a sample of unknown DNA with the profile produced from a sample known to belong to an identified individual. The laboratory then calculates a statistical probability that a match could take place purely by chance. The more sections match within the two samples, the higher the probability that the DNA belongs to the same individual. . . .

DNA Profiling in Law Enforcement

Law enforcement agencies around the world are increasingly relying on DNA evidence. Although DNA evidence alone can seldom be used to prove that an individual committed a crime, it can be used to place the individual at the crime scene if the scene contains biological evidence. When a DNA profile is derived from evidence at the crime scene, law enforcement officials can search forensic DNA databases for a matching DNA profile to determine whether the evidence came from an individual who committed a prior offence. They can also request DNA samples from suspects or, in some countries, conduct "DNA sweeps" of large numbers of people to find an individual whose DNA matches evidence found at the crime scene. In some cases, when the police have a suspect and know of locations where that individual's tissue samples may be stored, a search warrant may be used to obtain the sample for analysis. The high confidence placed in DNA matches makes it particularly important that biological evidence be handled carefully to avoid contamination and that other evidence be available to link the individual to the crime. DNA evidence has been challenged in courts of several countries because of improper handling during evidence collection or testing.

According to the 2002 global survey by Interpol, 77 of its 179 member countries perform DNA analysis and 41 member countries have forensic DNA databanks, which include both physical samples and databases of DNA profiles. The percentage of members having DNA databanks is predicted to double in the next few years. Interpol is in negotiations to create protocols for searching and sharing DNA profiles across borders as part of its larger initiative on digital communications between law enforcement authorities.

The rules for inclusion in forensic DNA databanks and the rules that govern access to data, physical specimen retention, and privacy protections vary from country to country. In countries that operate under federal systems, such as US and Australia, rules for forensic DNA databanks can vary from jurisdiction to jurisdiction. The United Kingdom has the largest forensic DNA databank, which holds over 2.5 million samples of those who have been charged with one of a list of offenses and, since April 4, 2004, those who have been arrested but not charged.

DNA Databanks in the United States

US law enforcement agencies use databases of DNA profiles, created by the states and linked through the FBI's Combined DNA Index System (CODIS). These profiles contain the analysis of 13 segments of non-coding DNA, i.e., DNA that does not contain information about predispositions or other characteristics, but varies from individual to individual. The CODIS system, authorized by Congress in 1994, allows law enforcement officials to exchange and compare DNA profiles at the local, state and national levels. As of April 2004, over 1.8 million profiles were accessible through CODIS. The samples on which DNA profiles are based, usually blood or saliva, are kept at forensic laboratories around the country. Samples are generally maintained for a long time in order to permit retesting if DNA profile evidence is challenged or as technology improves.

States in the US have different legislative requirements for inclusion in DNA databanks. All 50 states require sex offenders to provide DNA samples. In addition, some states require DNA samples from some or all felons, and many states include juveniles in their databanks. Samples of convicted of-

Protecting Genetic Information in an Age of DNA Databanking

Imagining a fair and protective system for using DNA evidence in the criminal justice system isn't all that difficult. . . . Upon overturning a conviction, volunteered DNA samples and profiles should be promptly destroyed, preserving the individual's presumptive innocence. For people convicted of serious violent offenses and beyond the reach of such exculpatory evidence, however, the trade-off between privacy and public interest may tilt toward favoring a DNA databanking system with strong privacy protections, including sample destruction after profiling and prohibitions on uses other than comparing profiles with those collected from crime scenes. . . .

Privacy is a zero-sum entity: The extension of law-enforcement authorities' genetic gaze comes directly at the expense of an individual's power to withhold such information. . . . Negligence in protecting the privacy of offenders and criminal suspects may acclimate a public to weak protections of genetic materials. As the predictive powers of genetic technologies are refined, this could have grievous consequences for everyone.

Jonathan Kimmelman, Nation,
November 27, 2000.

fenders, whose profiles are submitted to the CODIS database, are retained indefinitely. State laws vary about the length of time other samples are retained. In at least one case, an individual who had not been convicted is suing the state to demand the return of his DNA sample. Federal and state law enforcement authorities have urged their legislatures to expand the scope of DNA databases. . . .

Numerous Privacy Concerns with the Collection, Use, and Storage of Genetic Data

Use of DNA in law-enforcement activities is a subject of debate in the United States and other countries. Civil rights, including privacy rights, are at the heart of the debate.

- *Security of DNA databanks*: DNA databanks require appropriate safeguards for storage of physical samples, database security for DNA profile databases, and security mechanisms to protect the links between the two. This creates several potential points at which individual privacy can be violated and requires complex and multi-layered security arrangements, as well as appropriate audit and accountability measures. Members of Australian and Scottish law enforcement agencies objected to having DNA of police force members included in DNA databanks in part because they were concerned that security breaches could lead to compromise of police DNA profiles. (Police officers' DNA would be included in forensic databanks in order to eliminate from the investigation biological evidence belonging to officers on the scene. Police officers' fingerprints are routinely included in forensic fingerprint databases for the same reason.)

- *Re-use of DNA samples for research, education and planning*: Forensic DNA databanks have in some cases been used for research and education. Some have suggested that since tissue samples, which are the source of DNA profiles, contain all the information about individuals' predispositions to disease, they should be used for planning by correctional authorities. Such use of highly personal information without individual consent has been questioned because it is inconsistent with good information practices, which require that personal data be used for purposes for which it was collected or for which explicit informed consent has been obtained from each individual. While an argument can be made that those who have been convicted of a crime lose some of their civil rights, this cannot be said of those who were arrested but never convicted but whose DNA remained in forensic databanks. Although secondary purposes such as research might be accomplished with de-identified information, the Victorian Privacy Commissioner raised doubt that DNA information can ever be permanently de-identified, "given it is essentially comprised of identifiable material." As a result, he proposed that the purposes for which forensic DNA databanks can be used should be clearly defined and subject for public discussion in order to permit appropriate balance between various public policy goals.

- *Storage of DNA of individuals who have never been involved in a crime*: In some cases DNA has been collected from witnesses or others in order to eliminate them from police inquiries. DNA has also been collected from families of suspects in order to determine whether suspects should continue to be pursued. Since individuals may be reluctant to question the authority of police requesting a DNA sample, it is not clear that individuals can provide truly free informed consent to additional uses of their DNA even when they sign consent forms. If such DNA samples or profiles are included in forensic databanks, the databanks will include many people who have not been arrested or convicted of crimes, and the use of these people's DNA by law enforcement officials and researchers could compromise individual privacy.

- *Due process in collection of DNA evidence*: Most US jurisdictions do not require consent in order to obtain a DNA sample from someone convicted of a crime. In some countries, police are permitted to use necessary force to collect a sample when a convicted individual refuses to do so voluntarily. It is not clear how many jurisdictions restrict covert collection of DNA samples from suspects, e.g., from a drinking glass or a napkin. Associated Press reported in August 2003 that at least one judge in Iowa ruled that the police did not violate a man's rights when they derived his DNA from a fork and water bottle he had used and left behind. On the other hand, the UK's Human Genetics Commission and the Australian Law Reform Commission recommended that surreptitious collection of DNA be done only if permitted by a search warrant.

| "Compulsory profiling of qualified federal offenders can only be described as minimally invasive."

Law Enforcement DNA Databanks Do Not Threaten Medical Privacy

Diarmuid F. O'Scannlain

The FBI maintains a databank of certain people's DNA, genetic information which can implicate suspects in past or future crimes. In 2004, a prisoner claimed that his privacy was violated when authorities forced him to submit his DNA to be included in the database. Writing on behalf of the court in the resulting case, United States v. Kincade, *Diarmuid F. O'Scannlain declares in the following viewpoint that the criminal justice system has "special needs" that may justify restricting the privacy and other liberties of prisoners and parolees. According to O'Scannlain, the state's interest in deterring repeat offenders and solving crimes using DNA technology trumps the rights of criminals. Besides, O'Scannlain asserts, DNA profiling is a minimally intrusive procedure, and criminals do retain their right to pri-*

Diarmuid F. O'Scannlain, opinion in *United States v. Thomas Cameron Kincade*, U.S. Court of Appeals for the Ninth Circuit, No. 02-50380, August 18, 2004.

vacy against capricious or harassing searches. Diarmuid F. O'Scannlain has been a judge on the U.S. Court of Appeals for the Ninth Circuit since 1986.

As you read, consider the following questions:

1. What does "STR" stand for?
2. What are "special needs" cases, as explained by O'Scannlain?
3. According to the author, what constitutional safeguards protect the privacy of conditional releasees?

Pursuant to the DNA Analysis Backlog Elimination Act of 2000 ("DNA Act"), individuals who have been convicted of certain federal crimes[1] and who are incarcerated, or on parole, probation, or supervised release must provide federal authorities with "a tissue, fluid, or other bodily sample . . . on which a[n] . . . analysis of th[at sample's] deoxyribonucleic acid (DNA) identification information" can be performed. Because the Federal Bureau of Investigation ("the Bureau") considers DNA information derived from blood samples to be more reliable than that obtained from other sources (in part because blood is easier to test and to preserve than hair, saliva, or skin cells), Bureau guidelines require those in federal custody and subject to the DNA Act ("qualified federal offenders") to submit to compulsory blood sampling. [According to] *Federal Probation Joins the World of DNA Collection*, failure "to cooperate in the collection of that sample [is] . . . a class A misdemeanor," punishable by up to one year's imprisonment and a fine of as much as $100,000.

The FBI's DNA Databank

Once collected by a phlebotomist, qualified federal offenders' blood samples are turned over to the Bureau for DNA analy-

1. These include murder, voluntary manslaughter, aggravated assault, sexual abuse, child abuse, kidnapping, robbery, burglary, arson, and any attempt or conspiracy to commit such crimes.

sis—the identification and recording of an individual's "genetic fingerprint." Through the use of short tandem repeat technology ("STR"), the Bureau analyzes the presence of various alleles [genic variant's responsible for producing a particular trait] located at 13 markers (or loci) on DNA present in the specimen. . . .

Once STR has been used to produce an individual's DNA profile, the resulting record[2] is loaded into the Bureau's Combined DNA Index System ("CODIS")—a massive centrally-managed database linking DNA profiles culled from federal, state, and territorial DNA collection programs, as well as profiles drawn from crime-scene evidence, unidentified remains, and genetic samples voluntarily provided by relatives of missing persons. As of March 2004, CODIS contained DNA profiles drawn from 1,641,076 offenders and 78,475 crime scenes. . . .

CODIS can be used in two different ways. First, law enforcement can match one forensic crime scene sample to another forensic crime scene sample, thereby allowing officers to connect unsolved crimes through a common perpetrator. Second, and of perhaps greater significance, CODIS enables officials to match evidence obtained at the scene of a crime to a particular offender's profile. In this latter capacity, CODIS serves as a potent tool for monitoring the criminal activity of known offenders. Through March 2004, Bureau data indicated that CODIS has aided some 16,160 investigations nationwide—1,710 within the Ninth Circuit.

A Convict Refuses to Submit His DNA

On July 20, 1993, driven by escalating personal and financial troubles, decorated Navy seaman Thomas Cameron Kincade robbed a bank using a firearm. . . . [Eventually he] was sen-

---

2. CODIS records contain the DNA profile, an identifier for the agency that provided the DNA sample, a specimen identification number, and the name of the personnel associated with the analysis.

tenced to 97 months' imprisonment, followed by three years' supervised release. . . .

On March 25, 2002, Kincade's probation officer asked him to submit a blood sample pursuant to the DNA Act. He refused, eventually explaining that his objections were purely a matter of personal preference—in his words, "not a religious conviction." . . .

[In 2003] Kincade finally was forced to submit to DNA profiling. He persists in his challenge to the Act [on the grounds that it violates the Fourth Amendment].

Privacy, the Fourth Amendment, and "Special Needs"

While "[i]t would be foolish to contend that the degree of privacy secured to citizens by the Fourth Amendment has been entirely unaffected by the advance of technology," [*Kyllo v. United States* (2001)] we begin—as always—with first principles.

Pursuant to the Fourth Amendment, "[t]he right of the people to be secure in their persons, houses, papers, and effects, against unreasonable searches and seizures, shall not be violated, and no Warrants shall issue, but upon probable cause, supported by Oath or affirmation, and particularly describing the place to be searched, and the persons or things to be seized." . . .

The Court has [however] sanctioned several general search regimes that are free from the usual warrant-and-probable cause Requirements. . . .

[One] category of suspicionless searches is referred to as "special needs," and in recent years, the Court has devoted increasing attention to the development of the accompanying analytical doctrine. . . .

The Court applied special needs analysis in [*Griffin v. Wisconsin* (1987)]. . . .

On [the case's] eventual appeal to the Supreme Court, the Justices explained:

> A State's operation of a probation system, like its operation of a school, government office or prison, or its supervision of a regulated industry, likewise presents 'special needs' beyond normal law enforcement that may justify departures from the usual warrant and probable-cause requirements. Probation, like incarceration, is a form of criminal sanction imposed by a court upon an offender after verdict, finding, or plea of guilty. . . . [I]t is always true of probationers (as we have said it to be true of parolees) that they do not enjoy the absolute liberty to which every citizen is entitled, but only conditional liberty properly dependent on observance of special probation restrictions. . . .

Limitations on Criminals' Rights

[We first take] note of the well-established principle that parolees and other conditional releasees are not entitled to the full panoply of rights and protections possessed by the general public. Quite to the contrary, the Court has recognized that "those who have suffered a lawful conviction" are properly subject to a "broad range of [restrictions] that might infringe constitutional rights in free society," [*McKune v. Lile* (2002)] . . . in no small part due to the extraordinary rate of recidivism among offenders. . . .

These restrictions generally "are meant to assure that the [conditional release term] serves as a period of genuine rehabilitation and that the community is not harmed by the [releasee]'s being at large. These same goals require and justify the exercise of supervision to assure that the restrictions are in fact observed," [according to] *Griffin*. And whether they are initially legitimated as furthering a "special need," [*Griffin*] or recognized merely as serving the government's "'overwhelming interest' in ensuring that a [releasee] complies with those requirements and is returned to prison if he fails to do so," [*Pennsylvania Board of Probation and Parole v. Scott* (1998), quoting *Morrissey v. Brewer* (1972)] once such strictures are imposed and clearly noticed, they dramatically alter the relationship between the releasee and the government. For at bottom, they render all kinds of individual choices—choices that otherwise would be privately considered, privately determined, and privately undertaken—matters of legitimate government concern and investigation. As we recognized nearly thirty years ago [in *Latta v. Fitzharris* (1975)]:

> The purposes of the parole system give the parole authorities a special and unique interest in invading the privacy of parolees under their supervision. In order to fulfill his dual responsibilities for helping the parolee to reintegrate into society and evaluating his progress, and for preventing possible further antisocial or criminal conduct by the parolee, it is essential that the parole officer have a thorough understanding of the parolee and his environment, including his personal habits, his relationships with other persons, and what he is doing, both at home and outside it. It is equally important that this information be kept up to date. . . . Many of the [accompanying] restrictions relate to matters which the [releasee] might otherwise be entitled to preserve as private.

These transformative changes wrought by a lawful conviction and accompanying term of conditional release are well-recognized by the Supreme Court, which often has noted that conditional releasees enjoy severely constricted expectations of privacy relative to the general citizenry—and that the government has a far more substantial interest in invading their privacy than it does in interfering with the liberty of law-abiding citizens. . . .

Criminals Retain Some of Their Privacy Rights

Let us be clear: Our holding in no way intimates that conditional releasees' diminished expectations of privacy serve to extinguish their ability to invoke the protections of the Fourth

Amendment's guarantee against unreasonable searches and seizures. . . . A conditional releasee may lay claim to constitutional relief—just like any other citizen. Further, and without regard to the outcome of any such analysis, we reiterate Judge [Stephen] Trott's recent observation [in *United States v. Crawford* (2003)] that conditional releasees likewise "retain a right of privacy against government searches and seizures that are arbitrary, a right of privacy against searches and seizures that are capricious, and a right of privacy against searches and seizures that are harassing." [*Skinner v. Railway Labor Executives' Assn.* (1989) noted] that "[a]n essential purpose of a warrant requirement is to protect privacy interests by assuring citizens subject to a search or seizure that such intrusions are not the random or arbitrary acts of government agents." These safeguards amply shelter the conditional releasee's residual expectation of, and entitlement to, privacy. . . .

A Minor Intrusion

We must balance the degree to which DNA profiling interferes with the privacy interests of qualified federal offenders against the significance of the public interests served by such profiling.

As we have recognized, compulsory blood tests implicate the individual's interest in bodily integrity—"a cherished value of our society," [as stated in *Schmerber v. California* (1966)] Nonetheless, it is firmly established that "the intrusion occasioned by a blood test is not significant, since such 'tests are a commonplace in these days of periodic physical examinations and experience with them teaches that the quantity of blood extracted is minimal, and that for most people the procedure involves virtually no risk, trauma, or pain.'" [*Skinner*, quoting *Schmerber*.] . . .

For parolees and supervised releasees especially—individuals who while in custody have been lawfully subject to much more severe intrusions of their corporeal privacy than a sterile

A Senator Suggests Collecting DNA from Anyone Who Is Arrested

When police retrace the history of a serial predator after he is finally caught, they often find that he never had a prior criminal conviction, but *did* have a prior arrest. That means the only way they are likely to catch such a perpetrator after his first crime—rather than his tenth—is if authorities can maintain a comprehensive [DNA] database of all those who are arrested, just as we do with fingerprints. . . .

A recent study produced by the city of Chicago demonstrates the potential of arrestee DNA databases by analyzing the case of serial murderer and rapist Andre Crawford.

In early 1993, Crawford was arrested for felony theft. If [the collection of DNA from arrestees were allowed], DNA could have been taken from him at that time and kept in NDIS [National DNA Index System]. Because it was not, when Crawford murdered a 37-year-old woman later that year, although he left DNA at the scene, he could not be identified as the perpetrator.

Over the next six years, Crawford went on to commit a rape and to murder 10 more women. If his DNA sample had been taken and kept in NDIS after his March 1993 arrest, he could have been identified and arrested after his first murder. One rape would have been prevented, and those women would still be alive.

Jon Kyl, "DNA 'Fingerprints' Can Help Catch More Criminals, Earlier," John Kyl Newsletter, September 19, 2005.

blood draw conducted by a trained medical professional, and who therefore leave prison with substantially reduced sensitivities to such exposure—the DNA Act's compelled breach of their bodily integrity is all the less offensive.

At the same time, the DNA profile derived from the defendant's blood sample establishes only a record of the defendant's identity—otherwise personal information in which the qualified offender can claim no right of privacy once lawfully convicted of a qualifying offense (indeed, once lawfully arrested and booked into state custody). For, as we recognized in [*Rise v. Oregon* (1995)], "[o]nce a person is convicted of one of the felonies included as predicate offenses under [the DNA Act], his identity has become a matter of state interest and he has lost any legitimate expectation of privacy in the identifying information derived from blood sampling."

Dramatic Hollywood Fantasies

Both Kincade and his supporting amici passionately protest that because the government does not destroy blood samples drawn for DNA profiling and because such samples therefore conceivably could be mined for more private information or otherwise misused in the future, any presently legitimate generation of DNA profiles is irretrievably tainted by the prospect of far more consequential future invasions of personal privacy. Judge [Stephen] Reinhardt's dissent likewise maintains that in light of the "nightmarish" possibilities CODIS portends, we must act immediately to halt the program—before the wolf enters the fold, rather than after.

The concerns raised by amici and by Judge Reinhardt in his dissent are indeed weighty ones, and we do not dismiss them lightly. But beyond the fact that the DNA Act itself provides protections against such misuse,[3] our job is limited to resolving the constitutionality of the program before us, as it is designed and as it has been implemented. In our system of government, courts base decisions not on dramatic Hollywood fantasies but on concretely particularized facts devel-

---

3. It strictly limits the permissible uses of DNA profiles and stores samples and sets criminal penalties for violators.

oped in the cauldron of the adversary process and reduced to an assessable record. If, as Kincade's aligned amici and Judge Reinhardt's dissent insist, and when, some future program permits the parade of horribles the DNA Act's opponents fear—unregulated disclosure of CODIS profiles to private parties, genetic discrimination, state-sponsored eugenics, and (whatever it means) the use of CODIS somehow "quite literally, to eliminate political opposition"—we have every confidence that courts will respond appropriately. As currently structured and implemented, however, the DNA Act's compulsory profiling of qualified federal offenders can only be described as minimally invasive—both in terms of the bodily intrusion it occasions, and the information it lawfully produces.

"Children are being acclimated to violations by the state that their grandparents would have found unconscionable."

Drug Testing Violates Students' Privacy

Peter Cassidy

Peter Cassidy argues in the following viewpoint that random drug testing in schools humiliates students and violates their privacy rights. According to Cassidy, drug testing was originally enacted to ensure that conscripts and criminals remained sober, yet this intrusion is now being inflicted upon innocent schoolchildren. He laments that the Supreme Court has upheld the drug testing of students engaged in competitive extracurricular activities. This decision, he cautions, opens the door to future infringements on privacy, such as drug tests for all students, all drivers, or all voters. Peter Cassidy writes on national affairs, the law, and technology.

As you read, consider the following questions:

1. According to the author, what extracurricular activities will now be subjected to drug testing?

Peter Cassidy, "Pee First, Ask Questions Later," *In These Times*, January 20, 2003, p. 10. Reproduced by permission of the publisher, www.inthesetimes.com.

2. What Supreme Court decision set the stage for drug testing of the total student population, in Cassidy's view?

3. What does the author predict will happen in the next five to fifty years?

In the past decade [1993–2003], a veritable *Kindergulag* has been erected around schoolchildren, making them subject to arbitrary curfews, physical searches, psychological profiling schemes and—in the latest institutionalized indignity—random, suspicion-less, warrantless drug testing for just about any kid who wants to pursue extracurricular interests.

Last summer [2002], the Supreme Court gave *carte blanche* to school districts that want to impose drug testing on kids who've cast suspicion upon themselves by volunteering for extracurricular activities. The 5-to-4 decision on June 27 upheld a drug-testing program in a Tecumseh County, Oklahoma, school district that requires students engaged in any "competitive" extracurricular activities to submit to random drug testing.

Understanding the Supreme Court's Decision

This isn't just about keeping jocks from enjoying a post-practice beer or joint. The decision approves the testing of any student who volunteers for the Future Farmers of America, Future Homemakers of America, the cheerleading squad, the choir, the color guard or even those sacrosanct curators of Sousa, the marching band.

There is understandably a good deal of sympathy for drug testing as a social safety mechanism to catch kids who might be heading toward life-destroying drug abuse, social isolation and crime. Who doesn't want to catch a kid before he takes a lifelong fall? Yet before parents surrender their kids to the arms of the therapeutic enforcement state, they need to come to terms with the provenance of the interventions they are tacitly endorsing for their kids—and some of the more enduring shared consequences of drug testing.

Drug testing actually arrived in American schools by way of the armed forces and the prison system. The Navy began testing servicemen for drugs 30 years ago, when the first test kits were developed. By the late '70s, prisoners were being subjected to urinalysis. By the mid-'80s, defense-related contractors were pressed to test their work forces for purity. In the final days of the [Ronald] Reagan administration, the Federal Drug Free Workplace Act forced drug testing on all federal contractors working on projects of any appreciable size. From there, against sporadic and fractured opposition by labor unions and civil liberties groups, urinalysis and drug-testing programs proliferated in almost every industry.

America's kids are now being subjected to the kind of intrusions the nation would inflict only upon conscripts and criminals just 20 or 30 years ago. Who knows how much further it could go? The latest decision in *Board of Education of Independent School District No. 92 v. Earls* essentially opens the way for general random drug testing of America's entire school population, says Timothy Lynch, director of the Criminal Justice Project at the Cato Institute in Washington.

How Drug Testing Came to Schools

The first movement toward urinalysis of the total student population was choreographed by the Supreme Court in 1995 with the *Vernonia School District v. Acton* case in Oregon. The court decided, among other things, that since athletes shower together, they have little expectation of privacy—and thus urinalysis of athletes was deemed constitutional.

In the case of Lindsay Earls—who was humiliated after being yanked out of choir practice by Tecumseh school administrators and ordered to urinate on command (she tested negative)—the Supreme Court justices appeared eager to ex-

The Many Ways in Which Random Drug Testing Infringes on Students' Privacy

The Tulia Independent School District [in Texas] has seen a dramatic reduction in student participation in extracurricular activities since implementing drug testing. One female student explains:

> "I know lots of kids who don't want to get into sports and stuff because they don't want to get drug tested. That's one of the reasons I'm not into any [activity]. Cause . . . I'm on medication, so I would always test positive, and then they would have to ask me about my medication, and I would be embarrassed. And what if I'm on my period? I would be too embarrassed." . . .

[In another case,] when Tecumseh High School in Oklahoma enacted its random drug testing program, the school failed to ensure the protection of private information concerning prescription drug use submitted under the testing policy. The Choir teacher, for instance, looked at students' prescription drug lists and left them where other students could see them. The results of a positive test, too, were disseminated to as many as 13 faculty members at a time. Other students figured out the results when a student suddenly was suspended from his/her activity shortly after the administration of a drug test. This not only violates students' privacy rights, but can also lead to costly litigation. . . .

Students are taught that under the U.S. Constitution, people are presumed innocent until proven guilty and that they have a reasonable expectation of privacy. Random drug testing undermines both lessons; students are assumed guilty until they can produce a clean urine sample, with little regard given to students' privacy rights.

Fatema Gunja et al., Making Sense of Student Drug Testing: Why Educators Are Saying No, *ACLU and Drug Policy Alliance, January 2004.*

tend the scope of drug testing. In oral arguments last March [2002], Justice Anthony Kennedy taunted ACLU [American Civil Liberties Union] Attorney Graham Boyd, hypothesizing that his client would prefer to attend a "druggie" school.

Writing for the majority, Justice Clarence Thomas extended the relevance of the factors used to test "reasonableness" of a search in *Vernonia* to apply much more broadly, while enthroning the school district's interest in detecting drug use. In a breathtaking act of militant jurisprudence and shabby reasoning, Justice Thomas quickly expanded the universe of candidates for urinalysis and established a new entitlement for the state to determine the suitability of testing beyond parental guidance—"custodial responsibilities," he called it.

After the decision, scores of school districts immediately began inspecting the language of the decision and considering establishing their own urinalysis programs based on the Tecumseh model.

The Expansion of Drug Testing Is Inevitable

In the Lockney School District in West Texas, Superintendent Raymond Lusk told the *New York Times* in September [2002], "We'll probably get 85 percent of the kids in extracurriculars. I think it would be fairer to test everybody, because why are some kids more important than others?"

Touché. Now that there is a state entitlement to test at will, pressing the PC buttons that demand fairness in application of entitlements and social burdens will surely extend testing to all students.

The prognosis for the rest of us is just as grim. With the Supreme Court establishing that the state has a superseding interest in cultivating a therapeutic enforcement role that trumps even clear, constitutionally guaranteed freedoms, nothing should be ruled out of the realm of possibility. A drug test requirement when you renew your driver's license? For filing a tax return? Before you vote?

Give it five years—or 50. Children are being acclimated to violations by the state that their grandparents would have found unconscionable. The future Supreme Court justices being conditioned in our schools today will no doubt chuckle in disbelief some day that on-demand urinalysis was ever an issue of legal contention.

"A school's interest in protecting children from the influence of drugs outweighs their expectation of privacy."

Student Drug Testing Is Necessary

John P. Walters

As head of the Office of National Drug Control Policy, John P. Walters is the nation's drug czar in charge of fighting illicit drug use. In the following viewpoint he contends that students must be randomly drug tested in order to reduce the number of youths who abuse drugs. Drug testing is not a punishment, he insists, but is a way to identify and treat young drug users. Furthermore, Walters contests claims that random drug testing compromises students' privacy. The issue of privacy has in fact been carefully considered, he explains, and measures are in place to ensure that student drug test results are kept confidential. The benefits of student drug testing, he concludes, far outweigh privacy concerns.

As you read, consider the following questions:

John P. Walters, "Random Student Drug Testing Works. It's About Public Health—Identifying Individuals Who Need Help and Treatment—Not Punishment," *Pittsburgh Post-Gazette*, May 4, 2005. Reproduced by permission of the author.

1. How many fewer youths use drugs today than in 2001, according to Walters?
2. What is the government doing through regional summits, in the author's contention?
3. According to Walters, what were the results of the 2001 study in the *American Journal of Psychiatry*?

Over the past three years [2002–2005], youth drug use in America has declined by 17 percent. Today, there are 600,000 fewer young people using drugs than in 2001. While our prevention efforts are resulting in a national decline, too many young people are still using drugs. Pennsylvania is no exception. Our youth continue to use drugs, particularly marijuana, at an alarming rate. In fact, approximately 15 percent of Pennsylvanians between the ages of 12 and 17 tried marijuana in 2004, a startling statistic.

Drug Testing Helps to Fight Drug Abuse

We know from 20 years of experience that we are not powerless against drug use in America. There are proven methods to reduce the number of youth who start using drugs. In 2002, a promising solution emerged when the U.S. Supreme Court cleared the way for schools to perform random drug tests on a much larger portion of the student population [i.e., those who participate in competitive extracurricular activities].

That decision marked the beginning of a hopeful new phase in the effort to keep our children drug-free. Drug testing is not performed to punish students or expel them, but rather to identify individuals who need help, and to refer them to counseling or treatment.

The White House Office of National Drug Control Policy is holding a series of regional summits throughout the country (including one in Pittsburgh tomorrow [May 5, 2005]) for concerned education officials and community leaders to inform them about random student drug testing. Through these summits we are educating participants about developing student drug testing policies, legal considerations associated with starting and executing a program, technology used in administering random drug tests, the importance of a student assistance program and federal grant opportunities. The information offered at the summits is for schools and communities to use in determining if this prevention tool is appropriate for their needs.

Random student drug testing is not a federal mandate. Individual communities must determine their own response to addressing the unique challenges of drug abuse in their areas. For schools and communities weighing whether or not to implement a student drug testing program, a few facts merit consideration.

Many Americans still have antiquated notions about the dangers of marijuana, but research over the last decade [1995–2005] has proven the harmful effects of marijuana use, especially for youth. The National Institute on Drug Abuse notes that heavy marijuana use impairs the ability of young people to concentrate and retain information during their peak learning years. Additionally, the *American Journal of Psychiatry* published a study in 2001 presenting evidence that marijuana abusers are four times more likely to report symptoms of depression and have more suicidal thoughts than those who never used the drug.

Furthermore, numerous studies recently published by European researchers have shown a strong correlation between marijuana use and schizophrenia. Drug testing is an appropriate public health response, just as testing for tuberculosis in schools was a way of identifying and then limiting a public health epidemic.

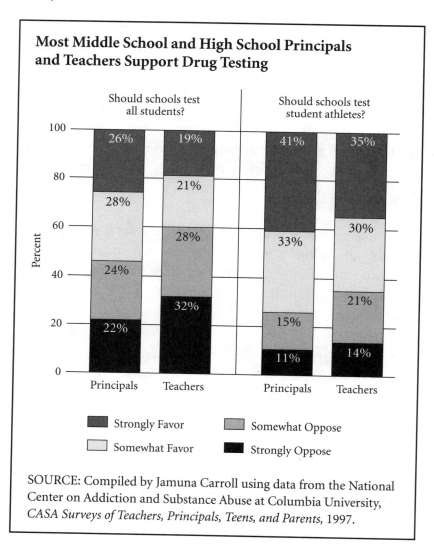

Most Middle School and High School Principals and Teachers Support Drug Testing

SOURCE: Compiled by Jamuna Carroll using data from the National Center on Addiction and Substance Abuse at Columbia University, *CASA Surveys of Teachers, Principals, Teens, and Parents*, 1997.

The Benefits of Drug Testing Outweigh Privacy Concerns

There are those who represent student drug testing as a tool of "Big Brother"[1] and a violation of personal privacy. Upon examination, these concerns have turned out to be largely un-

---

1. Big Brother is the fictional oppressive government described in George Orwell's *1984*.

founded and often exaggerated. The Supreme Court, in fact, carefully weighed the privacy issue, ultimately determining that a school's interest in protecting children from the influence of drugs outweighs their expectation of privacy. The court further mandated that the results of the tests be kept confidential—shared only with the parents of the student, in order to help refer the student into the appropriate level of counseling or treatment, not punishment.

To dwell on possible problems with drug testing is to overlook the potential benefits, which are enormous. Already, drug testing has proven remarkably effective at reducing drug use in schools and businesses throughout the country. As a deterrent, few methods work better or deliver clearer results. Drug testing of airline pilots and school bus drivers has made our skies and roadways much safer for travel. And since the U.S. military began testing in the early 1980s, drug use among servicemen and women has plunged from 27 percent to less than 2 percent.

Experience has taught us that people at the local level often know best how to deal with drug problems in their own communities. But to combat the threat, they need good information and the best resources available. These summits will provide parents, school administrators, teachers and mentors with the knowledge to consider drug testing as part of an overall strategy to fight drug use.

Periodical Bibliography

Janelle Brown — "Why Drug Tests Flunk," Salon.com, April 22, 2002. www.salon.com.

Peter Byrne — "Big Doctor Is Watching," *SF Weekly*, May 28, 2003.

Janlori Goldman — "Statement Before the U.S. Senate Special Committee on Aging," September 23, 2003. www.healthprivacy.org.

Jonathan Kimmelman — "Just a Needle-Stick Away: DNA Testing Can Convict the Guilty; It Can Also Destroy the Privacy of Millions," *Nation*, November 27, 2000.

Jon Kyl — "DNA 'Fingerprints' Can Help Catch More Criminals, Earlier," September 19, 2005. www.kyl.senate.gov.

Robert Pear — "Bush Rolls Back Rules on Privacy of Medical Data," *New York Times*, August 10, 2002.

Marsha Rosenbaum — "Random Student Drug Testing Is No Panacea," *Alcoholism & Drug Abuse Weekly*, April 12, 2004.

OPPOSING
VIEWPOINTS®
SERIES

CHAPTER 4

How Should Privacy Be Protected?

Chapter Preface

In recent years legislators have drafted hundreds of privacy bills in response to an upsurge in identity thefts, privacy violations over the Internet, and other activities that many Americans see as intrusions into their lives. One measure that some have called for is a law protecting genetic privacy. Genetic information contained in a person's DNA is specific to that individual. DNA can divulge, for instance, a person's risk of later developing certain medical conditions. Some fear that when this information is revealed to insurance companies, employers, or other entities, it may become the basis for discrimination.

Employees are one group that could face prejudice as a result of genetic testing, according to the Human Genome Project. HGP explains what kinds of discriminatory acts need to be legislated against:

> Based on genetic information, employers may try to avoid hiring workers they believe are likely to take sick leave, resign, or retire early for health reasons (creating extra costs in recruiting and training new staff), file for workers' compensation, or use healthcare benefits excessively. Some employers may seek to use genetic tests to discriminate against workers—even those who do not and may never show signs of disease.

Such was the case at Burlington Northern Santa Fe Railroad. The company tested its employees for a genetic condition that causes carpal tunnel syndrome, and also screened for maladies such as diabetes and alcoholism, without the workers' knowledge. One employee charged that he was discriminated against for refusing to undergo the exam—he was threatened with termination. To prevent such discrimation, genetic privacy expert George Annas calls for "no collection of DNA without the authorization of the individual. No DNA analysis—looking for specific genes or chromosomes—without informed consent of the individual. No disclosure to anyone of the results of the test without explicit authorization." He and others who protest genetic testing in the workplace fear that without protective legislation, workers could be illegally terminated based on confidential health information.

Other commentators respond that these fears are unwarranted. In a statement before the U.S. House of Representatives, Tom Miller of the Cato Institute alleged, "Evidence that employers try to obtain, let alone use, such information generally is limited to isolated anecdotes." Like others who oppose genetic privacy legislation, he believes a company has a right to know of factors that may adversely affect its employees' job performance, and workers should not be allowed to hide their genetic predispositions. Miller contends, "One's right to privacy should not include the right to misrepresent oneself to the rest of the world. . . . Employers should be able to seek whatever information they might find relevant to their employee's job performance." Corporations argue that economically, it makes sense to hire and retain workers who will probably remain healthy in the future. Healthier employees generally use less sick time and cost less to insure. Furthermore, some companies assert that genetic testing of job candidates is performed for their own safety. Doctors may screen for genetic characteristics that would increase an employee's risk if exposed to certain environmental conditions during work. As protection, employees who exhibit genetic predispositions for certain illnesses would not be permitted to work in those conditions.

People who favor genetic privacy legislation are opposed by others who feel such laws would be unwarranted and unfair. Indeed, many privacy laws are contested on the grounds that they are unnecessary, unconstitutional, or unhelpful. In the following chapter authors attempt to find a reasonable solution to America's privacy concerns.

> "Approximately 25 million individuals'
> information would be in the [military
> recruiting] database, and there is no
> way to opt out."

Military Recruiters Should Be Barred from Accessing Students' Information

Electronic Privacy Information Center

Two federal laws require high schools to hand over student information—such as names, addresses, and phone numbers—to military recruiters upon request. To give the military unimpeded access to youths' personal data is intrusive, argues the Electronic Privacy Information Center (EPIC) in the following viewpoint. In EPIC's contention, the Department of Defense uses the contact information to aggressively and deceptively recruit students and has compiled the information into a secret database, which violates the 1974 Privacy Act. Alarmingly, EPIC notes, schools that refuse to reveal students' information may lose their federal funding. EPIC, a public interest research center, disseminates information on privacy and civil liberties issues.

Electronic Privacy Information Center, "DOD Recruiting Database," October 13, 2005, www.epic.org. Reproduced by permission.

As you read, consider the following questions:

1. How did the Department of Defense violate the Privacy Act, in EPIC's contention?

2. What evidence does EPIC cite in support of its assertion that recruiters are too aggressive?

3. According to the author, what could result from schools' failure to comply with the Defense budget amendment?

In May 2005, the Department of Defense (DOD) announced that it was going to create a massive database for recruiting. The DOD's "Joint Advertising and Market Research" system proposed to combine student information, Social Security Numbers (SSN), and information from state motor vehicle repositories into a mega database housed at a private direct marketing firm. Approximately 25 million individuals' information would be in the database, and there is no way to opt out. In June 2005, EPIC [Electronic Privacy Information Center] and 8 privacy and consumer groups objected to the creation of the database, arguing that it violated the Privacy Act [of 1974] and was unnecessarily invasive.

In reaction to the EPIC comments and significant media attention, DOD held a media roundtable in June 2005 where the agency admitted that it had already created the database. This is a clear violation of the Privacy Act, which requires federal agencies to announce and seek public comment on systems of personal information before they are created. . . .

Protections from Military Recruiters Are Needed

We have laws to protect us against commercial telemarketers and spammers, but we don't have protections against military recruiters who engage in abusive marketing techniques. Voice of America reported that ". . . U.S. Army officials report more than 300 substantiated cases of allegedly improper recruiting tactics last year [2004], a 60% increase in 5 years. Many recruiters reportedly have resorted to aggressive tactics because they've had a hard time meeting the Army's recruiting quota of 2 enlistees a month." Recent headlines recount other abusive recruitment techniques; these techniques could become significantly more pervasive when the efficiencies of private-sector direct marketing techniques are brought to bear on those in the database. Indeed, just a few months ago, an Indiana National Guard recruiter's access to personal information was credited with his ability to efficiently target women for sexual assault: "Investigators say he [the recruiter] picked out teens and young women with backgrounds that made them vulnerable to authority. As a military recruiter, he had access to personal information, making the quest easier."

Two laws were passed in 2001 which make it easier for military recruiters to access high school students' contact information. The laws changed schools' previous ability, under the Family Educational Rights and Privacy Act (FERPA), to choose to whom they would release such information.

Under the FERPA, schools may release "directory" information about students, such as phone numbers and addresses, as long as parents or adult students have an opportunity to opt out of such disclosure at the beginning of the school year. This represents an exception to the FERPA's general restriction on the public release of student records, and was meant to provide schools with the ability to publish students' names in honor rolls, yearbooks and the like, and to provide contact information to outside groups like class ring companies. Schools, or their districts or boards, have traditionally decided what directory information would be released, for what purposes, and to what groups.

However, a provision inserted into the No Child Left Behind educational act, Section 9528, now *requires* public and private schools receiving federal educational funds to release secondary students' names, addresses and telephone numbers to military recruiters who request them. Parents or students may request that the information not be released to recruiters, often by signing a form distributed by schools early in the school year. Even if a school or district previously had a policy of not releasing directory information to outside groups, or even particularly to the military, it must now allow military recruiters to access the information of any students who are not opted out of such disclosure.

Section 9528 also requires schools receiving federal funds to provide the "same access" to its secondary students as it provides to colleges or prospective employers. This presumably means, for instance, that schools would have to allow military recruiters to attend a school-sponsored job fair.

The amendment was introduced by Representative David Vitter (R-La), and was agreed to overwhelmingly by Congress. Congress also legislated near-identical requirements in a provision of the 2002 Defense Department budget authorization bill.

The Schools Respond

The requirements of Section 9528 and the Defense budget amendment went into effect in the 2002 school year, and they quickly inspired widespread objections. Students protested in Hackensack, NJ, in January 2003. The Eugene, Oregon, school district distributed forms stating that although it would comply with the laws, it did not support them. And the San Francisco school board adopted a resolution responding to the requirements that began: "Whereas: Soul music legend Curtis Mayfield said: 'We got to have peace/To keep the world alive and war to cease.'"

In October 2002, The New York Civil Liberties Union [NYCLU] appealed to the Chancellor of New York City's education department to require written permission to release student information to the military. The group wrote: "Opt-out features typically receive little attention or response, which means information will be released by default, rather than in-

Electronic Privacy Information Center, www.epic.org. Reproduced by permission.

tention." Although New York City's schools did not adopt the NYCLU suggestion, school districts throughout the country, including the San Francisco school district, did choose to automatically withhold student information from recruiters unless students or parents requested otherwise. The Departments of Education and Defense, however, stated in response that it would not allow such a practice. In a July 2003 letter to various school districts, the Departments wrote that schools may not refuse to disclose student information to the military by default, but may only withhold students' information if they have been notified of this preference by the students or their parents. In practice, this will mean that in schools where forms are distributed for students or parents to opt out of information-release to military recruiters, an unreturned form will result in disclosure to interested recruiters.

Since the Departments of Education and Defense issued their letter, the San Francisco school board has modified its policies to comply with the Departments' interpretation of the laws.

If a school or district fails to comply with Section 9528, it could lose future federal funding and could even be asked to return funds that it already received from the government. Almost all public schools and many private schools receive federal educational funds. Failure to comply with the similar Defense budget amendment could result in a visit to the school from a senior military officer, and, later, notification of the breach to the governor or even to Congress. The Department of Education wrote in a frequently asked questions document that when a report is made to Congress "the expectation is that public officials will work with the LEA [local educational agencies] to resolve the problem."

Preserving Students' Privacy

If high school students, or their parents, do not want names, addresses or phone numbers released to military recruiters, they must be sure to fill out and return any opt out form that their school provides regarding military recruiters. Under the Department of Education's interpretation of the law, an unreturned form is supposed to indicate that a student's information may be released. In addition, students or parents may want to encourage their school or school district to provide a way to specifically opt out of disclosure of directory information to military recruiters without having to deny release of such information generally. Schools are required, under FERPA, to allow parents or adult students to opt out of the general release of directory information for listings such as yearbook and honor roll, and high school students may prefer to allow release of their information for this use, but not for military recruitment.

The creation of the database caused many to revisit public policy choices made by Congress on military recruiting. As explained above, under the No Child Left Behind law, Congress forced public and private schools receiving federal educational funds to release secondary students' names, addresses and telephone numbers to military recruiters who request them.

Representative [Mike] Honda (D-CA) introduced H.R. 551, the Student Privacy Protection Act of 2005 in February to reverse this presumption. If passed, it would require affirmative consent before personal information is transferred from schools to recruiters.[1]

The legislation would not address the practice of recruiters buying personal information from direct marketing companies, or limit recruiters' access to personal information held by state motor vehicle departments.

---

1. The bill was still in Congress as this volume went into print.

"*Providing [student directory] information [to the military] is consistent with
the Family Educational Rights and
Privacy Act.*"

Military Recruiters Should Be Permitted to Access Students' Information

*Part I: Rod Paige and Donald H. Rumsfeld; Part II: Michael
Turner*

*In the following two-part viewpoint, government officials main-
tain that the military needs access to students' contact information in order to encourage youths to join the military. Part I is a
letter sent by Rod Paige, former U.S. Secretary of Education, and
Donald H. Rumsfeld, Secretary of Defense, to all state departments of education. According to Paige and Rumsfeld, recruiters
should be able to inform secondary school students that the military offers youths a college education, scholarships, and experiences that foster valuable skills. In Part II U.S. Representative
Michael Turner from Ohio laments that colleges have banned*

Part I: Rod Paige and Donald H. Rumsfeld, "Joint Letter from Secretary Paige and Secretary Rumsfeld," October 9, 2002. www.ed.gov. Part II: Michael Turner, "Equal Access
for Military Recruiters at Institutions of Higher Education," February 18, 2005.
www.house.gov.

military recruiters from their campuses. In his view, the military should be given the same access to students as any other prospective employer, and students can ignore enlistment offers if they wish.

As you read, consider the following questions:

1. According to the authors of Part I, what act protects the privacy of students' educational records?
2. Name two schools that ban military recruiters from their campuses, according to Michael Turner.
3. In Michael Turner's opinion, when is the government and national security endangered?

For more than 25 years, the Armed Forces of our Nation have been staffed entirely by volunteers. The All-Volunteer Force has come to represent American resolve to defend freedom and protect liberty around the world. Sustaining that heritage requires the active support of public institutions in presenting military opportunities to our young people for their consideration.

Recognizing the challenges faced by military recruiters, Congress recently passed legislation that requires high schools to provide to military recruiters, upon request, access to secondary school students and directory information on those students. Both the *No Child Left Behind Act of 2001* and the *National Defense Authorization Act for Fiscal Year 2002* reflect these requirements.

In accordance with those Acts, military recruiters are entitled to receive the name, address, and telephone listing of juniors and seniors in high school. . . . Providing this information is consistent with the *Family Educational Rights and Privacy Act*, which protects the privacy of student education records. Student directory information will be used specifically for armed services recruiting purposes and for informing young people of scholarship opportunities. For some of our students, this may be the best opportunity they have to get a college education.

The support by our Nation's educational institutions on behalf of the U.S. Armed Forces is critical to the success of the All-Volunteer Force. It can be, and should be, a partnership that benefits everyone. As veterans, and as Cabinet Members serving the President, we can attest to the excellent educational opportunities the military affords, as well as an environment that encourages the development of strong character and leadership skills.

Recently, I voted with an overwhelming, bipartisan majority of my House colleagues to support a House Resolution expressing the continued support of Congress for equal access for military recruiters at institutions of higher education.

Unbelievably, this resolution was needed because a significant number of institutions of higher education decided to ban military recruiters from their campuses. Who would imagine that our colleges and universities, which receive federal funds, would claim they need to "protect" their adult students from the influences of US military recruiters? Yale Law School, for example, recently announced such a ban in a decision announced in a school-wide email. Harvard University also bars military recruiters.

Laws Governing Military Recruiting

Yale began banning military recruiters from its campus on the heels of a Third Circuit Court of Appeals decision that ruled against the Department of Defense actively enforcing the 1995 Solomon Amendment. The Solomon Amendment blocks federal funding to schools that ban military recruiters from campus. Congress passed the amendment to safeguard military recruiting. The amendment links federal funding of educational institutions to the willingness of those schools to provide access by military recruiters to campuses and students. This ac-

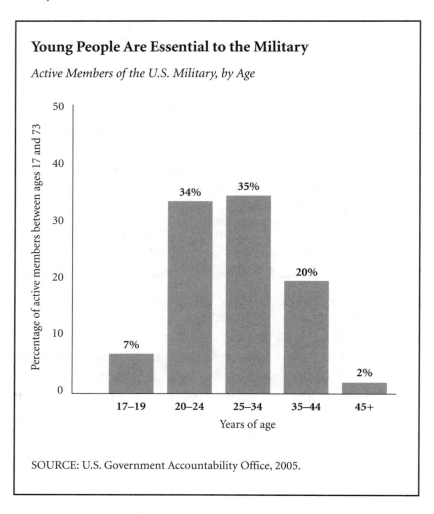

Young People Are Essential to the Military

Active Members of the U.S. Military, by Age

SOURCE: U.S. Government Accountability Office, 2005.

cess must be at least equal in quality and scope to that provided to other prospective employers.

Article I, Section 8 of the Constitution specifically provides Congress with the power to raise and support armies and maintain a Navy, and make rules for the government and regulation of the land and naval forces. The Nation's security interests, especially during these difficult times, require a high level of military personnel readiness and thus, effective recruitment programs.

Compelling Interests

College and university campuses are among the most important locations for military recruitment. The same colleges that would stand in line for federal funding should not be able to turn away recruiters from the Armed Forces or any other branch of the federal government. Once on campus, the recruiters have no more rights or persuasive powers than any other potential employer and the student has the right to contract their future service with whom they choose, in the free market system.

Following all federal policies is a responsibility that comes with accepting federal funding. When institutions fail to allow military recruiters onto campuses on an equal basis with other potential employers, the government, and thus national security, including the potential personal security of every American family, are endangered. Schools that ban military recruiters are harming our nation's military readiness and preparedness.

It is ironic that the Third Circuit Court of Appeals, which ruled in favor of a coalition of law schools and professors who were suing the Department of Defense, found that the Solomon Amendment "is not narrowly tailored to advance a compelling government interest and thus unjustifiably burdens the faculty members' First Amendment right of expressive association."

I can think of no government interest more compelling than protecting the country, which requires raising suitable Armed Forces. Further, faculty members need not have any expressive association with the Armed Services or any other employer, just as no student need have any association. Each potential employer on campus represents an option each student can choose to accept or ignore in the free market of ideas.

This case may ultimately be decided by the Supreme Court. However, my House colleagues and I have weighed in with overwhelming bipartisan support for a resolution expressing the continued support of Congress for equal access for military recruiters to institutions of higher education, as well as reaffirming our support for the Solomon Amendment enacted by Congress a decade ago.

| "Laws against homosexuality interfered with the most private aspects of consensual adult relations."

Allowing Same-Sex Marriage Would Protect Privacy Rights

Don Knowland

In the viewpoint that follows, Don Knowland proposes that laws barring gays from having sex or getting married violate their right to make their own personal decisions. The state, Knowland asserts, should not interfere with Americans' private, consensual sexual interactions, nor should it impose moral standards on gay citizens who have done no harm. Permitting homosexuals to marry, he suggests, would offer them the same rights and privileges as other Americans. Knowland writes for the World Socialist Web site, which is hosted by the International Committee of the Fourth International, a socialist group that aims to unite the world's working class in its struggle for equality.

As you read, consider the following questions:

1. What does Knowland say is the purpose of the proposed federal marriage amendment?

Don Knowland, "Ballot Initiatives Seek to Bar Same-Sex Marriage," World Socialist Web Site, November 2, 2004. Reproduced by permission.

2. According to the author, what legal rights are bestowed to married people?

3. In Knowland's view, which constitutional rights were denied to interracial couples before the *Loving* decision?

On November 2 [2004], election ballots in eleven US states, including Michigan, Ohio, Georgia and Oregon, will include initiatives to outlaw same-sex marriage. Other states, such as Missouri, have already voted such bans into their constitutions.

The [George W.] Bush administration last February [2004] came out in support of a federal constitutional amendment that would define marriage solely as "a union between a man and a woman." The proposed amendment is designed to prevent individual states from recognizing same-sex marriages.[1]

Such an amendment would nullify the recent ruling of the Massachusetts Supreme Court, which held that denying marriage to same-sex couples violated their constitutional right to equal protection under the law and their fundamental right to marry whomsoever they pleased. Under that ruling, gays have been free to marry in Massachusetts since May.

The Socialist Equality Party [SEP] opposes all efforts to limit the rights of gay persons, including the right of same-sex couples to marry. Involved here is a basic question of democratic rights and equality under the law. The SEP opposes any and all measures that discriminate against people on the basis of race, gender or sexual orientation.

Unfair Limitations on the Right to Marry

In the case of laws against same-sex marriage, anti-gay discrimination and bigotry combine with an anti-democratic and unconstitutional promotion of religious conceptions as the

---

1. In November 2005 a similar amendment was being considered by the Senate Committee on the Judiciary.

The Marriage Resolution

Because marriage is a basic human right and an individual personal choice, RESOLVED, the State should not interfere with same-gender couples who choose to marry and share fully and equally in the rights, responsibilities, and commitment of civil marriage.

LAMBDA GLBT (Gay Lesbian Bisexual Transgender) Community Services, "The Marriage Resolution." www.lambda.org.

basis for public policy—something that violates the separation of church and state laid down in the First Amendment of the US Constitution. Ultimately, the arguments supporting a ban on same-sex marriage rest on religious beliefs, which, according to the Constitution, may not be enshrined as law.

The institution of marriage is itself the product of a particular historical and social evolution. Limiting marriage by law to one of its historical forms, in order to discriminate against a section of society, is fundamentally reactionary, whether it takes the form of a ban on marriage between gays, or, as was the case not so long ago in parts of the US, prohibits marriage between people of different races. . . .

Denying marriage to adults of the same sex has very concrete repercussions. Marriage laws provide for rights to inherit and distribute property after death, for care of children and adults, and protections in other important spheres of life.

Most recent polls show that while most people claim they do not object to what adults, including homosexuals, do in the privacy of their homes, most also oppose same-sex marriage. For many, democratic instincts are in conflict with religious teachings, which are whipped up by reactionary politicians. Undoubtedly, many who oppose gay marriage reflect a fear that homosexual conduct will be promoted by putting the stamp of approval on gay unions. . . .

The legal views expressed by the Supreme Court in the 1967 *Loving v. Virginia* decision [which struck down Virginia's law banning interracial marriage] are highly relevant to the current debate over gay marriage. The court stated that "the freedom to marry has long been recognized as one of the vital personal rights essential to the orderly pursuit of happiness by free men," such that the Virginia statute deprived interracial couples of their liberty without due process of law, in violation of the Fourteenth Amendment of the US Constitution.

The Supreme Court further argued that the Virginia statute also violated the equal protection clause of the Fourteenth Amendment, and noted that it "had consistently repudiated distinctions between citizens solely because of their ancestry as being odious to a free people whose institutions are founded upon the doctrine of equality."

Even under limited principles of bourgeois equality before the law, there can be no credible argument that persons should be deprived of the basic civil right to marry whomever they choose because of an inclination toward those of the same sex, no more so than because of the accident of their ancestry. The Massachusetts Supreme Court reasoned in precisely that fashion this year [2004] in granting same-sex couples the constitutional right to marry.

For the Massachusetts court to arrive at its ruling, the US Supreme Court had first to reverse its fifteen-year-old ruling that a state (Georgia, in that case) could constitutionally prosecute homosexuals for engaging in sodomy. [In 2003,] the US Supreme Court did just that. In the *Lawrence* [*v. Texas*] case, it ruled that Texas's anti-sodomy statute violated the equal protection and due process rights of homosexuals. Justices Anthony Kennedy and Sandra Day O'Connor, considered the conservative "swing vote" justices on the Court, wrote concurring opinions essentially conceding that the Court's view only

15 years before was rooted in backward prejudice against homosexuals, much like prejudice against women or blacks in the past.

Gay Marriage and Privacy

The ruling in *Lawrence* emphasized that laws against homosexuality interfered with the most private aspects of consensual adult relations. Such considerations of fundamental privacy rights argue strongly as well for recognition of gay marriages. The right to privacy is an expression of the more general democratic and legal proposition that the state does not have a right to impose a moral standard on individuals, except to prevent actions that harm others, e.g., criminal actions such as theft, homicide, fraud and the like.

Ruling classes have long used religious conceptions and base prejudices to obscure the workings of society and divert exploited classes from struggle against their exploiters. The campaign against same-sex rights is such an attempt, this time by the most reactionary sections of the American ruling elite.

"[Allowing] gay marriage . . . is a case of judicial activism run amok, for the contemporary right to privacy has its roots precisely in the traditional definition of marriage."

The Right to Privacy Does Not Extend to Same-Sex Marriage

James Taranto

Some lower courts, citing Americans' right to marital and sexual privacy, have permitted gay couples to marry. In the following viewpoint James Taranto insists that such decisions are misguided and rest on shaky legal ground. Whether or not to allow same-sex marriage is not a privacy issue, he avers. Taranto is the editor of OpinionJournal.com, hosted by the Wall Street Journal. *He also authors the daily Best of the Web Today column.*

As you read, consider the following questions:

1. In Taranto's opinion, which court decision introduced the right to reproductive privacy?

2. Who authored the *Casey* decision?

3. How does Taranto explain the case against same-sex marriage?

Last week [in February 2005] a state judge held that New York City's refusal to issue marriage licenses to same-sex couples violates the constitutional right to privacy. When the Massachusetts Supreme Judicial Court mandated the recognition of same-sex marriage in 2003, it too cited the right to privacy. Whatever the merits of gay marriage, this is a case of judicial activism run amok, for the contemporary right to privacy has its roots precisely in the traditional definition of marriage.

"Would we allow the police to search the sacred precincts of marital bedrooms for telltale signs of the use of contraceptives?" Justice William O. Douglas asked rhetorically in the 1965 U.S. Supreme Court case of *Griswold v. Connecticut*. Then he answered: "The very idea is repulsive to the notions of privacy surrounding the marriage relationship."

But the court did not long confine those "notions of privacy" to "the marriage relationship." In less than a decade it expanded the right of *marital* privacy into a right of *reproductive* privacy. In *Eisenstadt v. Baird* (1972) the court held that unmarried couples have the same right as married ones to obtain and use contraceptives, and the following year, in *Roe v. Wade*, the justices declared that the right to privacy includes abortion.

In 1986 the justices refused to take the next step of recognizing a right to *sexual* privacy. In *Bowers v. Hardwick*, they upheld a state law prohibiting homosexual sodomy between consenting adults. But in 1992 the Supreme Court set the stage for overturning *Bowers*. In *Planned Parenthood v. Casey* —a decision for which Justices Sandra Day O'Connor, Anthony Kennedy and David Souter claimed joint authorship— the court essentially upheld *Roe*, while asserting a new, breathtakingly expansive formulation of the right to privacy.

Gay Marriage Is Not an Issue of Privacy

No doubt someone will bring a lawsuit demanding that the Supreme Court find a constitutional right for gay people, like straight people, to wed a partner of their choice. But this would not be a privacy suit. It would be an equal-protection suit, saying that states should not discriminate in the granting of marriage licenses.

Jonathan Rauch, National Journal, *July 26, 2003.*

"Intimate and personal choices," the justices wrote [in *Casey*], are "central to the liberty protected by the Fourteenth Amendment. At the heart of liberty is the right to define one's own concept of existence, of meaning, of the universe, and of the mystery of human life." Justice Kennedy cited this language in his majority opinion in *Lawrence v. Texas*, the 2003 case that found sodomy laws were unconstitutional after all.

The U.S. Supreme Court has not yet taken up the question of same-sex marriage. But as Justice Antonin Scalia argued in his *Lawrence* dissent, it's hard to see how one could square a ban on same-sex marriage with what he mockingly called "the famed sweet-mystery-of-life passage" [from *Casey*, cited above]. If the Constitution guarantees no less than the right to "define one's own concept of . . . the universe," how can government limit the definition of marriage to a man and a woman, or for that matter limit it at all? (Justice O'Connor argued in *Lawrence* that "preserving the traditional institution of marriage" is in fact a "legitimate state interest," but it's telling that none of the other five justices in the majority joined her concurrence.)

Same-Sex Marriage Is Not a Privacy Issue

None of these cases rest on solid legal ground. As Justice Douglas acknowledged in *Griswold*, the right to privacy is to be found not in the Constitution but in its "penumbras" and "emanations." At the same time, there is a strong political consensus against the government intruding into people's bedrooms. If *Griswold* and *Lawrence* disappeared from the books tomorrow, it's unlikely any state would rush to re-enact laws against contraceptives or consensual sodomy.

Abortion and same-sex marriage, by contrast, do spark strong opposition, but not on privacy grounds. Abortion opponents argue that life before birth is worthy of legal protection, while the case against same-sex marriage is that it confers public approval on gay relationships—approval the New York and Massachusetts courts have given without public consent.

When judges find rights in hidden constitutional meanings, they run a twofold risk. If they limit those rights, striking balances and compromises between such competing values as privacy vs. life or privacy vs. morality, they act as politicians, only without democratic accountability. The alternative, to let those rights expand without limit, seems more principled and thus is more appealing. But it ignores democracy's most important principle of all: the right of the people to govern themselves.

"Companies that buy and sell data operate with little oversight and, therefore, have little impetus to protect personal information."

Data Brokers Must Be Regulated to Prevent Identity Thefts

Nikki Swartz

Data brokers gather the personal information of millions of Americans and sell it to companies and government agencies. In the viewpoint that follows, Nikki Swartz claims that these information brokers operate with few regulations. As a result, data brokers have little incentive, she claims, to protect confidential information from identity thieves—criminals who use other people's names, Social Security numbers, and other personal data to obtain goods and services. Federal laws governing the distribution of private information should focus on preserving confidentiality and should require data brokers to notify citizens if their records may have been compromised, Swartz writes. Swartz, a freelance writer, is the former associate editor of the Information Management Journal.

Nikki Swartz, "Database Debacles," *Information Management Journal*, vol. 39, May–June 2005, pp. 20 (4). © 2005, ARMA International. Reproduced by permission.

As you read, consider the following questions:

1. In Swartz's contention, what kinds of organizations are allowed to subscribe to ChoicePoint's services?
2. According to the *New York Times*, what actions likely result in a consumer's information being stored in a database?
3. What legislation is in Colorado's Senate, as cited by the author?

In March [2005] LexisNexis, a worldwide leader in global legal and business data, discovered that thieves had stolen data—including names, addresses, and Social Security and drivers' license numbers—on up to 310,000 U.S. consumers.

[This and other recent] incidents have raised new warnings about companies that sell private data and their growing banks of personally identifiable information pertaining to millions of individuals' lives. Many, including lawmakers, are now saying the data-broker industry has too little government oversight and contending that such databases should fall under regulations that govern credit reports.

The ChoicePoint and LexisNexis Calamities

ChoicePoint, one of the largest information brokers, revealed that scammers posing as legitimate Los Angeles–area businesses opened 50 fraudulent accounts and accessed various databases used for pre-employment background checks and public records searches.

They paid fees of $100 to $200 and provided fake documentation to identify their businesses as insurance agencies, check-cashing companies, and other organizations that would have normally been allowed to subscribe to ChoicePoint's services. After setting up accounts and gaining access to Choice-Point databases, thieves were able to gather a treasure trove of information—including addresses, phone and Social Security numbers, credit files, and even names of relatives and neighbors—on at least 145,000 people. Investigators said they believe up to 400,000 individuals' records may have been compromised, but ChoicePoint contends that the breach affected only about 145,000 personal records, some of which are duplicates.

According to police records, the account holders then made unauthorized address changes on at least 750 people. This is a trick identity thieves often use to establish credit accounts that they can use to make fraudulent charges. However, it is not clear whether any false charges were made in these specific cases before the fraud was discovered.

U.S. investigators alerted ChoicePoint to the security breach in October 2004, but the company did not send out notification letters to its 30,000 consumers in California—the only U.S. state that requires database firms to notify consumers of a security breach—informing them that their privacy had been breached until late February 2005. . . .

Recently, LexisNexis, a company that provides searches of legal and business data, discovered that cyber criminals had hacked into its computer systems and stolen data files on as many as 310,000 U.S. customers. The stolen files included names, addresses, Social Security numbers, and driver's license information. The information was stolen from Seisint, a LexisNexis subsidiary. LexisNexis detected the security lapse in a review of procedures at Seisint.

The Dangers of Data-Mining

The commercial data-broker industry collects and sells information for profit. ChoicePoint, for example, aggregates data on millions of Americans from hundreds of sources. The reports are then sold to thousands of companies and government agencies that want to learn more about their clients, customers, or employees.

ChoicePoint has acquired more than 50 companies since its founding in 1997 and now has access to 19 billion records.

Its customers include Fortune 500 companies, insurance agencies, corporate employee screeners, check-cashing companies, media outlets, private investigators, law enforcement agencies, and the U.S. government.

According to *The New York Times*, "if a person has held a job, held a lease, obtained a driver's license, carried a credit card, been fingerprinted, taken a drug test, gone to court, or simply received mail," it is likely that all that information and much more is stored in one or more consumer databases and available for sale.

Westlaw, another information database company, provides the Social Security numbers of millions of Americans to its subscribers. Its "People-Find" feature allows some Westlaw users to type in any name and receive personal data about that individual, including addresses and Social Security numbers, that have been culled from public records. Sen. [Charles] Schumer [D-N.Y.] called it an "egregious" invitation to identity theft. Westlaw said Social Security information is restricted to government agencies and a small number of corporations that need it, such as insurance companies.

There are hundreds of data brokers like Westlaw, and consumers have no way of knowing what information such companies possess and whether it is protected. The LexisNexis Group provides information services to legal, media, government, and academic markets. Acxiom, another data broker, serves the financial services, insurance, direct marketing, publishing, retail, and telecommunications industries.

Existing Laws Are Inadequate

Companies that buy and sell data operate with little oversight and, therefore, have little impetus to protect personal information. Existing laws do not help consumers protect themselves in a world where private information is collected in huge databases and then bought and sold with minimal rules or restrictions.

Recommendations of the Federal Trade Commission Regarding Data Brokers

Recent security breaches have raised questions about whether data brokers and other companies that collect or maintain sensitive personal information are taking adequate steps to ensure that the information they possess does not fall into the wrong hands, as well as about what steps should be taken when such data is acquired by unauthorized individuals. . . .

The [Federal Trade] Commission recommends that Congress consider whether companies that hold sensitive consumer data, for whatever purpose, should be required to take reasonable measures to ensure its safety. Such a requirement could extend the FTC's existing GLBA [Gramm-Leach-Bliley Act of 1999] Safeguards Rule to companies that are not financial institutions.

Further, the Commission recommends that Congress consider requiring companies to notify consumers when the security of this information has been breached in a manner that creates a significant risk of identity theft.

Federal Trade Commission, statement before the Committee on Commerce, Science, and Transportation, U.S. Senate, June 16, 2005.

The biggest problem may be that not one but many legal and government authorities oversee the commercial collection and distribution of private information. According to the *Times*, current laws were not created to address, and do not regulate, "the current power of data gatherers to amass and distribute vast digital dossiers on ordinary citizens." State and federal regulators and lawmakers are now calling for those rules to be updated.

Among the pertinent federal rules are the following:

- The Fair Credit Reporting Act of 1970 and its 2003 version, the Fair and Accurate Credit Transactions Act, establish rules for access to and distribution of consumer reports and requires credit report providers to vouch for the accuracy of their information.
- The 1994 Drivers Privacy Protection Act protects driving records.
- The Health Insurance Portability and Accountability Act of 1996 addresses the privacy of medical records.
- The Gramm-Leach-Bliley Act of 1999 governs the use of personal information collected by financial institutions.

State laws differ from state to state, sometimes conflict, and are highly inconsistent in the degree to which they protect the privacy of their residents. According to the *Times*, state laws have not kept pace with the emergence of data-mining companies because they focus too much on industry-specific uses of information such as credit reports or medical data rather than on protecting the privacy of individuals whose information is in the databases.

Californians seem to be the best-protected U.S. residents. It was that state's unique law that prompted the disclosure of the ChoicePoint breach.

More Regulations on the Horizon

The ChoicePoint theft has grabbed the attention of lawmakers. Two Senate committees have held hearings to review the situation, and the Federal Trade Commission (FTC) is investigating whether ChoicePoint complied with federal consumer safety data regulations.

Members of Congress have called for investigations and new legislation to better regulate the data-brokering industry. Sen. Dianne Feinstein (D-Calif.) said, "existing laws no longer suffice when thieves can steal data not just from a few victims at a time but from thousands of people with vast, digitized efficiency." She introduced three consumer privacy bills in January [2005][1], including one that would create a national version of California's security breach notification law. Another would give U.S. residents the right to know if their personal information has been stolen and used to commit a crime.

Several states, including Georgia, New York, and Texas, are considering similar laws. Legislation working its way through the Colorado Senate would make notification mandatory and allow consumers to put a "freeze" on their credit reports, which would make it difficult for anyone to access them without the consumer's permission.[2]

Rep. Joe Barton (R-Texas), chairman of The U.S. Committee on Energy and Commerce, has directed his staff to investigate the storage and security practices of database companies. *The Wall Street Journal* reported that Sen. Bill Nelson (D-Fla.) will introduce legislation that would extend the provisions of the Fair Credit Reporting Act to govern commercial data brokers, giving the FTC jurisdiction over companies like Choice-Point.

Such a law would give consumers broad new protections. U.S. residents would be entitled to review data stored on data brokers' computers once annually for free and to correct any errors. Consumers would also be able to see a list of companies that have requested a look at their personal information.

MSNBC.com reported that Nelson and House member John Conyers (D-Mich.) will call for the General Accounting Office to investigate government contracts with commercial data brokers.

Outrage over the recent high-profile data breaches may result in passage of a national notification law, which would re-

---

1. As this volume went into publication, no major action had been taken on these bills.

2. A bill allowing credit report freezes passed and will go into effect in July 2006.

quire data brokers to notify individuals at risk following a data theft.

ChoicePoint, meanwhile, has said it will start restricting who can buy the data it collects to reduce the likelihood that identity thieves will gain access to its databases. But for hundreds of thousands of consumers, the damage may have been done already.

| "The current patchwork of local
[stalking] laws barely protects some
[cyberstalking] victims, while altogether
neglecting others."

A Federal Law Criminalizing Cyberstalking Is Needed

Harry A. Valetk

Cyberstalking is a form of harassment in which a perpetrator repeatedly contacts a victim through e-mail, instant messaging, or other Internet systems. In the following viewpoint Harry A. Valetk warns that the absence of a clear federal cyberstalking law results in a plethora of conflicting state laws that sometimes leave victims without protection. Because state statutes vary widely in their definition and punishment of cyberstalking, Valetk claims, law enforcement is hesitant to get involved in these cases. Federal cyberstalking legislation, he opines, would better protect victims. Harry A. Valetk, who practices law in New York, works with parents, teachers, and law enforcement to help victims of cybercrimes.

As you read, consider the following questions:

1. What are many cyberstalking victims urged to do, although it is seldom enough, according to the author?
2. How does stalking legislation in Massachusetts differ from that of Minnesota and Texas, in Valetk's contention?
3. In the author's view, what is the key to a successful cyberstalking prosecution?

"Help! Is there any way to find out the identity of a person sending threatening and harassing instant messages to my 15-year-old daughter?" wrote one distressed mother from Seattle.

Another desperate victim asked, "This guy named Raul on Yahoo message boards has been making threats about raping me and then killing me. Is there anything I can do about that?"

Unfortunately, the Internet's low cost, ease of use, and anonymous features have given criminals a fascinating new place to misbehave. And, as more of us make the Internet our home within our homes, more predators are misusing new technology to harass, terrorize and stalk victims like never before.

Today, cyberstalking is a growing global concern that remains largely ignored.

What Is Cyberstalking?

Although no universal definition exists, cyberstalking occurs when an individual or group uses the Internet to stalk or harass another. Online, stalking involves repeated attempts to contact someone on the Internet using e-mail, chat rooms, bulletin boards or instant messages. Often, cyberstalkers also use their technical skills to misuse confidential information available online about their victims.

But, unlike any other means, the Internet also allows cyberstalkers to incite others against their victims. By impersonating the victim, a cyberstalker can cleverly send lewd e-mails to employers, easily post inflammatory messages on multiple bulletin boards and simultaneously offend hundreds of chat-room participants. The victim is then banned from bulletin boards, accused of improper conduct and flooded with threatening messages from strangers.

Worst of all, for many victims, cyberstalking typically means enduring terror for months before seeking help. And, even after they decide to ask for help, few know where to turn. The lucky ones find refuge in non-profit Internet safety organizations like Wiredpatrol. Since many local police departments lack the proper training and resources to investigate cyberstalking cases, however, many victims are urged simply to contact their Internet service provider [ISP] or "shut off" their computers.

But shutting off a computer is seldom enough. Cyberstalking is a serious crime that serves as a prelude to offline-stalking. Frequently, the danger is real, and the consequences of neglect are tragic. In 2001, for example, a Massachusetts man was sentenced to five years in prison after he pleaded guilty to stalking and raping a 14-year-old girl he met in a chat room.

Many Conflicting State Laws

Ironically, despite the elusive, multi-jurisdictional nature of cyberstalking, no uniform federal law exists to protect victims or define ISP liabilities. Instead, federal law imposes a $1,000 fine or five years imprisonment for anyone transmitting in interstate commerce any threat to kidnap or injure the person of another.

But, the absence of a clearly defined cyberstalking crime at the federal level forces states to draft their own legislation. Not surprisingly, the result is a complicated maze of state laws that offer varying definitions, protections and penalties.

How You Can Protect Yourself Against Cyberstalking

- Do not share personal information in public spaces anywhere online, nor give it to strangers, including in e-mail or chat rooms. Do not use your real name or nickname as your screen name or user ID. Pick a name that is gender- and age-neutral. And do not post personal information as part of any user profiles.

- Be extremely cautious about meeting online acquaintances in person. If you choose to meet, do so in a public place and take along a friend.

- Make sure that your ISP [Internet Service Provider] and Internet Relay Chat (IRC) network have an acceptable use policy that prohibits cyberstalking. And if your network fails to respond to your complaints, consider switching to a provider that is more responsive to user complaints.

- If a situation online becomes hostile, log off or surf elsewhere. If a situation places you in fear, contact a local law enforcement agency.

- If you are receiving unwanted contact, make clear to that person that you would like him or her not to contact you again.

U.S. Department of Justice, Cyberstalking: A New Challenge for Law Enforcement and Industry, *August 1999.*

At last count, 41 U.S. states had laws expressly prohibiting harassing conduct through the Internet, e-mail or other electronic means. In some states, such as New York, cyberstalking is part of the general stalking or harassment laws, while other states, such as North Carolina, have a separate section under special computer crime legislation. The general stalking or harassment laws of other states may be construed to cover cyberstalking without expressly stating that the Internet or e-mail is also covered. Still, the current patchwork of local laws barely protects some victims, while altogether neglecting others.

This is a real problem. In practice, conflicting state statutes—riddled with complex jurisdictional issues—deter law enforcement from ever getting involved. To illustrate, consider that Arizona's stalking statute only prohibits credible threats of violence against the victim, whereas California and South Carolina prohibit threats against the victim's immediate family. In Maine, a stalker's course of conduct can constitute an implied threat. But what legal standard applies to a cyberstalker from Maine, terrorizing an Arizona resident, using a California ISP?

Without a doubt, differing statutory definitions serve mostly to confuse everyone involved. To be guilty of cyberstalking in Massachusetts, the perpetrator must have an intent to cause "imminent fear." While in Minnesota and Texas, the perpetrator must only have knowledge that he or she is causing fear. That's why a victim's responses to the e-mails or electronic communications can be important.

Most states require direct communication with the target or family, but Wisconsin only requires sending a message that the person is likely to receive. A common example would be a list messaging service.

Most states also require that threats be against the person receiving the e-mail, while Washington goes so far as to prohibit threats against "any other person." North Dakota's statute goes even further, defining harassment to include a threat to inflict injury on a person's reputation. Others include obscenity, lewd, or profane language, but are usually tied with intent to harass. Another group of states include damage to property within the meaning of cyberstalking or cyber-harassment.

Among the most generous definitions, Arizona's statute simply requires that a victim be "seriously alarmed" or "annoyed." Illinois's statute prohibits spreading viruses in the same legislation. Some increase the offense from a misdemeanor to a felony if there were prior similar contacts with the victim, or prior similar bad acts. A few states increase the penalty if the offender is a convicted felon. Wisconsin is similar to Arkansas, but also prohibits anonymous e-mail or other actions that attempt to prevent disclosure of identity, if made with intent to harass.

Prevention

Given the varying standards, users should keep a full record of all harassing e-mail. In some States, authorities must first see if consent was given or whether the person requested that the contact stop. Some states require more than one communication or contact before pronouncing the activity illegal. Also, in states where e-mail contact is only one of several methods of harassment or stalking, even one e-mail might help show that the contacts were "repeated" or frequent enough to violate anti-cyberstalking statutes. Bottom line, victims must resist their natural impulse to delete offensive or threatening messages. In most cases, the key to a successful cyberstalking prosecution is to preserve the full electronic evidence trail.

In sum, there's little presently available to protect Internet users against a cyberstalker's demented obsession. Even worse, until a uniform federal criminal standard exists, victims can only hope that they live in a state that at least has some legislation on the subject.

"Restricting information flows to protect privacy . . . inevitably imposes costs on consumers, businesses, and the economy as a whole."

Privacy Protection Laws Are Unnecessary and Unconstitutional

Fred H. Cate

Privacy legislation too often has severe drawbacks, according to law professor Fred H. Cate in the following viewpoint. For one thing, he maintains, privacy laws stifle the open flow of information that is necessary to sustain the economy, preserve democracy, prevent crime, and meet customers' needs. He notes that privacy legislation may result in high costs for consumers and businesses, deny consumers access to services, and impede law enforcement. Furthermore, he argues, such laws are often unconstitutional because they restrict the free expression of companies and generally do not address a specific and significant harm to Americans. Fred H. Cate authored Privacy in the Information Age.

Fred H. Cate, "Protecting Consumer Privacy: Ten Questions Every Legislator Should Ask," *The National Retail Federation,* September 16, 2000, pp. 1–5. Reproduced by permission.

As you read, consider the following questions:

1. What point does the author make regarding laws that purport to protect personal data from private parties but not the government?
2. Name four benefits of information-sharing, as cited by Cate.
3. According to the author, the Court has struck down legislation restricting the publication of what types of information?

New laws to protect privacy are seldom necessary and often constitutionally forbidden. Thanks to a well-established array of state and federal privacy laws, an expanding competitive market for privacy protections, and new technologies and services that make real privacy a reality for the first time ever, additional legislation is rarely necessary.

Unfortunately, this has not deterred state and federal legislators from introducing more than 800 new privacy laws [from 1999 to 2000 alone]. Legislators and citizens are increasingly being called on to evaluate an avalanche of new privacy bills, many of which threaten the benefits that result from open information flows, would impose significant costs on consumers and businesses alike, and offer little enhanced protection for personal privacy.

Effective Privacy Law

As both a practical and a constitutional matter, new privacy legislation should respond effectively to a specific harm, interfere as little as possible with individual rights and competitive markets, impose the least cost consistent with the level of privacy protection provided, and be easy and intuitive to use. But it is not always easy to figure out which legislation meets these requirements, especially in the face of so many proposed bills.

These ten questions are designed to help legislators and citizens alike critically evaluate proposed privacy laws:

1. *Does the proposed law address a real problem?* This requires both that there be a real problem and that the law respond to it effectively. If the law's proponents don't identify a specific harm, be suspicious.

2. *Does the proposed law duplicate the protection provided by existing federal or state laws or regulations?*

3. *Is existing privacy law being enforced vigorously?* Proposals for new laws often obscure the fact that existing laws aren't being enforced. Enacting new privacy laws costs the government far less than enforcing existing ones, but does nothing to protect the public.

4. *Are the law's proponents addressing the cost of the proposed law explicitly and honestly?* That cost includes not only the expenses associated with implementing and complying with the law, but also its broader economic impact on consumers, businesses, and the economy. It is irresponsible to adopt a law without understanding the full range of costs it imposes. Distrust any proposal that does not include an estimate of its total economic impact.

5. *Does the proposed law create more problems than it solves?* What are the unintended (or intended, but unspoken) side-effects? Is the solution worse than the problem?

6. *Are the law's proponents making impossible claims for the proposed law?* Some advocates of new privacy laws claim that proposed laws will "give consumers control over their own information." These claims are seldom true and their vagueness suggests that the proponents of such laws may not have a clear idea of what harm they are trying to prevent. If a claim sounds too good to be true, it probably is. This is particularly true when a state law is offered as a solution to a national or international problem.

7. *Does the proposed law claim to protect personal information only from private parties or does it also restrict the*

government's collection and use of personal information? Laws that exempt the government from privacy protections are seldom effective or fair. Remember, the constitutional right to privacy only applies against the government; public officials and candidates should get their house in order first before telling others what to do. Question the credibility of any privacy law advocate who does not personally follow the same standards he or she is trying to impose on others.

8. *Does the proposed privacy law take away citizen choice?* The most basic privacy principle, recognized in every set of "fair information principles," is *choice* —the individual's right to make his or her own choice about the proper balance between the value of the open flow of information and the value of enhanced privacy protection, and to act on that choice by choosing among different levels and means (and corresponding costs) of privacy protection in the market. Privacy laws have the effect of denying consumers access to services and benefits that we value; those laws that make everyone pay for a high level of privacy that only a few desire should be avoided.

9. *Is the proposed law consistent with the Constitution?* Laws that would violate the Constitution, no matter how noble their purpose, are never good laws. The process of debating and enacting them wastes legislatures' time and the public's money. According to the U.S. Court of Appeals for the Tenth Circuit in *U.S. West, Inc. v. Federal Communications Commission* [1999], a decision the Supreme Court declined to review:

   a. laws restricting the collection and use of personal information to protect privacy restrict speech and therefore are subject to First Amendment review;

b. under the First Amendment, the government bears the burden of proving that its rules are constitutional;

c. that constitutional burden requires the government to demonstrate that its rules prevent a *"specific and significant harm "*; and

d. that the rules reflect "a 'careful calculat[ion of] the costs and benefits associated with the burden on speech imposed by its prohibition.' 'The availability of less burdensome alternatives to reach the stated goal signals that the fit between the legislature's ends and the means chosen to accomplish those ends may be too imprecise to withstand First Amendment scrutiny.'"

10. *Does the law reflect a serious approach to privacy?* Is the proposed law based on inaccurate facts or faulty expectations? Laws that respond to (or worse, encourage) public hysteria, exaggerate the harms they are intended to address or their likely effectiveness in addressing those harms, or fail to provide practical solutions to real problems serve the interests of politicians or advocacy groups, but not of the public.

These questions are by no means exhaustive, but they provide a critical first step toward assuring that proposed privacy laws are necessary, effective, appropriate, and constitutional. Enacting laws that do not meet these criteria threatens not only consumer convenience and economic prosperity, but our very liberty. . . .

The Cost of Privacy Protection

There is no question that privacy is important, both as a political issue and as a basic need of all people. Privacy is critical to our participation in this society and democracy; it is key to the growth and success of commerce online and off; and it is a topic of concern to many people today, as poll after poll demonstrates.

However, *restricting information flows to protect privacy—as each of the more than 800 legislative proposals identified above would have done—always, inevitably imposes costs on consumers, businesses, and the economy as a whole.* Often those costs are quite significant.

This should come as no surprise to anyone: *Information is the lifeblood of our 21st century economy.* In the words of the Federal Reserve Board: "[I]t is the freedom to speak, supported by the availability of information and the free-flow of data, that is the cornerstone of a democratic society and market economy." Efforts to restrict the flow of information—for whatever purpose—inevitably impose costs on us all. Those costs include both the substantive costs of greater privacy (*e.g.*, the costs associated with obscuring relevant information in commercial and personal transactions, impediments to law enforcement, and bad decisions and inefficiencies resulting from inadequate information), and the transaction costs of complying with new privacy laws. Perhaps the greatest costs of privacy, however, are the benefits of responsible information-sharing that we no longer enjoy.

The Benefits of Information-Sharing

Laws designed to protect privacy threaten the significant, practical benefits that open information flows bring. Those benefits are shared both by each consumer about whom data are shared and by all consumers in the aggregate because, as Federal Reserve Board Governor Edward Gramlich testified before Congress in July 1999, "[i]nformation about individuals' needs and preferences is the cornerstone of any system that allocates goods and services within an economy." The more such information is available, he continued, "the more accurately and efficiently will the economy meet those needs and preferences." *Without reliable access to personal information, neither government nor business can anticipate and meet citizen and consumer needs, and service and convenience suffer as a result.*

Information Sharing Saves Customers Time and Money

Customers of financial services companies obtain significant benefits from information sharing, including increased convenience, personalized service, and real savings of time and money. . . .

U.S. customers provide information to their financial institutions because they trust them to protect that information and use it wisely. To the extent these companies share customer information with affiliates and/or third parties, the information sharing provides customers with more services at lower prices, and allows the companies to increase efficiency, lower costs, and pass savings forward to customers.

Ernst & Young LLP, Customer Benefits from Current Information Sharing by Financial Services Companies, *December 2000.*

Information-sharing:

- makes it possible to ascertain customer needs accurately and meet those needs rapidly and efficiently;

- expands consumer access to a wide range of affordable services and products;

- significantly reduces the cost of many products and services;

- enhances customer convenience and services;

- improves efficiency;

- allows consumers to be informed rapidly and at low cost of those opportunities in which they are most likely to be interested;

- prevents and detects fraud and other crimes; and
- promotes competition by facilitating the entry of new businesses into competitive markets, smaller businesses competing more effectively with larger ones, and the emergence of new, specialized businesses. . . .

Constitutional Requirements

Enacting laws that restrict information without enhancing privacy protection or that fail to anticipate and explicitly consider the cost of privacy protection hurts consumers, businesses, and the entire economy. But such laws also raise constitutional issues. When the government restricts information flows—for whatever purpose—it must do so as narrowly or, in some cases, in the least restrictive way possible. Under this standard, the Court has struck down laws restricting the publication of confidential government reports, and of the names of judges under investigation, juvenile suspects, and rape victims.

Even if the information is considered to be "commercial," its collection and use is nevertheless protected by the First Amendment. The Supreme Court has found [in *Central Hudson Gas & Electric Corp. v. Public Service Comm'n* (1980) and *Board of Trustees v. Fox* (1989)] that such expression, if about lawful activity and not misleading, is protected from government intrusion unless the government can demonstrate a "substantial" public interest, the intrusion "directly advances" that interest, and is "narrowly tailored to achieve the desired objective."

The Supreme Court has long held that the constitutional protections for privacy—which, to start with, only apply against the government, not private parties—protect *reasonable* expectations of privacy and only then if necessary to prevent *specific harms*. When evaluating wiretaps and other seizures of private information under the Fourth Amendment, the Supreme Court has long asked whether the data subject in fact expected that the information was private and whether that expectation was reasonable in the light of past experience and widely shared community values. There should be no interference with information flows to protect privacy interests that are not reasonable.

To be reasonable, courts have held that *an expectation of privacy could not attach to public information.* No expectation of privacy may be reasonable if it involves information that is routinely and voluntarily disclosed or is available publicly. This reflects not only the Supreme Court's interpretation of the Fourth Amendment, but also the common sense that the law should not create costly or burdensome impediments to the collection and use of information that consumers willingly disclose and that is widely available in the marketplace.

Specific Harm

The law has also historically required that the government protect privacy interests *only when a specific harm is actually threatened.* This was the view of the U.S. Court of Appeals for the Tenth Circuit in *U.S. West, Inc. v. Federal Communications Commission.* The court's decision, which the Supreme Court declined to review, struck down the Federal Communications Commission's "opt-in" rules ... requiring that telephone companies obtain affirmative consent from their customers before using data about their customers' calling patterns to market products or services to them. The court wrote:

> In the context of a speech restriction imposed to protect privacy by keeping certain information confidential, the government must show that the dissemination of the information desired to be kept private would inflict *specific and significant harm* on individuals such as undue embarrassment or ridicule or intimidation or harassment or misappropriation of sensitive personal information for the purposes of assuming another's identity. Although we may feel uncomfortable knowing that our personal information is

circulating in the world, we live in an open society where information may usually pass freely. A general level of discomfort from knowing that people can readily access information about us does not necessarily rise to the level of substantial state interest under *Central Hudson* [the test applicable to commercial speech] for it is not based on an identified harm.

This principle is justified not only by the need to avoid unnecessary restraints on valuable information flows, but also because it is only by identifying the harm that a law is designed to prevent or remedy that a legislator, reviewing court, or citizen can judge whether the law is necessary and whether it does, in fact, respond to that harm. The harm principle has largely been lost in the flood of proposed privacy legislation.

Periodical Bibliography

Jennifer Barrett
"Testimony Before the House Committee on Energy and Commerce, Subcommittee on Commerce, Trade, and Consumer Protection: 'How Do Businesses Use Customer Information: Is the Customer's Privacy Protected?'" July 26, 2001. http://energycommerce.house.gov.

Brian Bergstein
"ID Theft Fears Overblown," Associated Press, November 13, 2005.

Richard A. Clarke
"You've Been Sold," *New York Times Magazine*, April 24, 2005.

Jim Harper
"Understanding Privacy—and the Real Threats to It," CATO Policy Analysis, August 4, 2004. www.cato.org.

Stanton McCandlish
"EFF's Top 12 Ways to Protect Your Online Privacy," Electronic Frontier Foundation, April 10, 2002. www.eff.org.

Phyllis Schlafly
"Your Privacy Is on the Chopping Block," *Conservative Chronicle*, October 9, 2002.

Michael Sivy, Pat Regnier, and Carolyn Bigda
"What No One Is Telling You About Identity Theft," *Money*, July 1, 2005.

Stacy A. Teicher
"No-Fly Zones for Military Recruiters," *Christian Science Monitor*, August 18, 2005.

Christine Wyatt Wood
"The Sodomy Decision," RenewAmerica, July 25, 2003. www.renewamerica.us.

For Further Discussion

Chapter 1

1. Laurie Thomas Lee researches privacy law, while Peter
    M. Thomson works for the Department of Justice. She
    believes that the Patriot Act infringes on privacy rights;
    he asserts that the government's need to protect citizens
    from terrorism justifies some privacy invasions. How do
    you think these authors' credentials may be affecting
    their view of the Patriot Act?

2. Ben Shapiro notes that people who do not want their
    bags to be searched by police can opt not to take the
    subway. Those who oppose random searches counter that
    this is an unreasonable suggestion because most people
    who take public transit have no other form of transporta-
    tion. Should all travelers be subjected to searches as a
    condition of using public transit? In what situations
    might it be reasonable to violate privacy? Explain your
    answer.

3. According to Charles Levendosky, criminals could obtain
    national ID cards using fraudulent documents, just as
    they do to receive driver's licenses today. However,
    Betty Serian insists that officials are being better trained
    to detect fake records and that security measures will
    ensure that people prove their identity before receiving
    their card. Do you believe that a national ID card would
    preserve privacy better than regular IDs do? Why or why
    not?

Chapter 2

1. To determine the privacy concerns of most Americans,
    Joseph Turow surveyed adults who use the Internet at
    home. In contrast, William F. Adkinson Jr., Jeffrey A.

Eisenach, and Thomas M. Lenard relied on a study in which researchers visited commercial Web sites and examined their privacy policies. What do you think are some potential problems with each survey's methodology? Which results do you find more credible, and why?

2. Gus Arroyo maintains that a video camera monitoring a public place is no different than a police officer waiting in an area and watching out for crime. However, Benjamin J. Goold thinks the difference is notable. With which author do you agree? Do you feel video surveillance is an unfair invasion of privacy, or is it an important crime prevention tool? Explain your answers.

3. After reading the viewpoint by Privacy International and the American Civil Liberties Union, do you find privacy concerns regarding biometrics reasonable? Or do you agree with the International Civil Aviation Organization that the security of biometric information will be protected? Explain.

4. Do you feel that employers are justified in monitoring workers? If so, under what circumstances? If not, why? Support your answer using facts from the viewpoints.

Chapter 3

1. The U.S. Department of Health and Human Services (HHS) claims that the Health Insurance Portability and Accountability Act of 1996 (HIPAA) enhances state laws, many of which provide greater privacy protections than does federal law. According to HHS, HIPAA will continue to do so even after it has been amended. Barry K. Herman and Deborah C. Peel fear, however, that as a result of the HIPAA amendments federal law will replace state laws as states eventually reduce or eliminate privacy protections. Whose prediction is more plausible, in your opinion? Why?

2. Peter Cassidy fears that if students are tested for drugs before being permitted to engage in extracurricular activities, the testing of all students—as well as voters and drivers—will eventually occur. Do you think that Cassidy's unease is justified? Or do you agree with John Walters' assertion that drug testing of certain students is necessary, and that this need trumps individuals' privacy rights? Support your answer using facts from the viewpoints.

3. Diarmuid F. O'Scannlain suggests that privacy concerns about the FBI's DNA databank are based on Hollywood fantasies. Electronic Privacy Information Center maintains that such fears are quite valid. After examining the evidence offered by each author, do you believe that DNA databases threaten privacy? Explain, using facts from the viewpoints.

Chapter 4

1. The Electronic Privacy Information Center is a public interest research center that distributes information on emerging privacy and civil liberties issues. Rod Paige, Donald H. Rumsfeld, and Michael Turner are all government leaders. How might these authors' credentials be affecting their views on whether military recruiters should be granted access to students' information?

2. Do you agree with Don Knowland's contention that marriage is a private, personal decision that homosexuals should be allowed to make, or do you believe James Taranto's assertion that the right to privacy does not encompass gay marriage? Explain your answer.

3. The measures proposed by Nikki Swartz and Harry A. Valetk would allegedly protect the privacy of consumers and cyberstalking victims. However, Fred H. Cate contends that such restrictions would be costly, would restrict the open flow of information, and would violate the

Constitution. After carefully considering these arguments, what, if any, privacy laws would you support? Why?

Organizations to Contact

American Civil Liberties Union (ACLU)
125 Broad St., 18th Fl., New York, NY   10004-2400
(212) 549-2500
e-mail: aclu@aclu.org
Web site: www.aclu.org

The ACLU is a national organization that works to defend civil rights as guaranteed in the Constitution. It publishes various materials on civil liberties, including the triannual newsletter *Civil Liberties*, and a set of handbooks on individual rights. "What's Wrong with Public Video Surveillance?" and "Answers to Frequently Asked Questions About Government Access to Personal Medical Information" are two of its articles.

The Brookings Institution
1775 Massachusetts Ave. NW, Washington, DC   20036
(202) 797-6000 • fax: (202) 797-6004
e-mail: brookinfo@brook.edu
Web site: www.brookings.org

The institution, founded in 1927, is a think tank that conducts research and education in foreign policy, economics, government, and the social sciences. In 2001 it began America's Response to Terrorism, a project that provides briefings and analysis to the public and which is featured on the center's Web site. Other publications include the quarterly *Brookings Review*, periodic *Policy Briefs*, and books such as *Terrorism and U.S. Foreign Policy*.

CATO Institute
1000 Massachusetts Ave. NW, Washington, DC   20001
(202) 842-0200 • fax: (202) 842-3490
e-mail: cato@cato.org
Web site: www.cato.org

CATO is a nonpartisan public policy research foundation dedicated to limiting the role of government and protecting individual liberties. It publishes the quarterly magazine *Regulation*, the bimonthly *Cato Policy Report*, and numerous policy papers and articles. "Understanding Privacy—and the Real Threats to It," and "Why Canning 'Spam' Is a Bad Idea" are among its works.

Electronic Frontier Foundation (EFF)
P.O. Box 170190, San Francisco, CA 94117
(415) 668-7171 • fax: (415) 668-7007
e-mail: eff@eff.org
Web site: www.eff.org

EFF is an organization that aims to promote a better understanding of telecommunications issues. It fosters awareness of civil liberties issues arising from advancements in computer-based communications media and supports litigation to preserve, protect, and extend First Amendment rights in computing and telecommunications technologies. EFF's publications include the quarterly newsletter *Networks & Policy*, the biweekly electronic newsletter *EFFector Online*, and online bulletins.

Electronic Privacy Information Center (EPIC)
1718 Connecticut Ave. NW, Suite 200, Washington, DC 20009
(202) 483-1140 • fax: (202) 483-1248
e-mail: info@epic.org
Web site: www.epic.org

As an advocate of the public's right to electronic privacy, EPIC sponsors educational and research programs, compiles statistics, and conducts litigation pertaining to privacy and other civil liberties. Its publications include the biweekly electronic newsletter *EPIC Alert* and a plethora of online reports, such as "National ID Cards and REAL ID Act."

Federal Aviation Administration (FAA)
800 Independence Ave. SW, Washington, DC 20591

(800) 322-7873 • fax: (202) 267-3484
Web site: www.faa.gov

The Federal Aviation Administration is the component of the U.S. Department of Transportation whose primary responsibility is the safety of civil aviation. The FAA's major functions include regulating civil aviation to promote safety and fulfill the requirements of national defense. Its International Flight Information Manual page contains links to terrorism-related information.

Federal Bureau of Investigation (FBI)
935 Pennsylvania Ave. NW, Room 7972, Washington, DC
   20535
(202) 324-3000
Web site: www.fbi.gov

The FBI, the principal investigative arm of the U.S. Department of Justice, investigates specific crimes assigned to it and provides other law enforcement agencies with cooperative services, such as fingerprint identification, laboratory examinations, and police training. The mission of the FBI is to uphold the law through the investigation of violations of federal criminal law and to protect the United States from foreign intelligence and terrorist activities in a manner that is faithful to the U.S. Constitution. Press releases, congressional statements, and major speeches are available on the agency's Web site.

Federal Trade Commission (FTC)
600 Pennsylvania Ave. NW, Washington, DC 20580
(877) 382-4357
Web site: www.consumer.gov

The Federal Trade Commission (FTC) works to ensure that the nation's markets are vigorous, efficient, and free of restrictions that harm consumers. The FTC enforces federal consumer protection laws that prevent fraud, deception, and unfair business practices, and combats identity theft, Internet scams, and telemarketing fraud. Publications posted on the FTC Web site offer consumer information concerning telemarketing, credit cards, and identity theft.

Health Privacy Project
1120 Nineteenth St. NW, 8th Fl., Washington, DC   20036
(202) 721-5632 • fax: (202) 530-0128
e-mail: info@healthprivacy.org
Web site: www.healthprivacy.org

Founded in 1997, the Health Privacy Project is dedicated to raising public awareness of the importance of ensuring health privacy in order to improve health care access and quality, both on an individual and a community level. The project provides research studies, policy analyses, Congressional testimony, and other information for those concerned with health care issues. It publishes fact sheets, editorials, press releases, privacy regulations guides, and reports on health privacy.

Heritage Foundation
214 Massachusetts Ave. NE, Washington, DC   20002
(202) 546-4400 • fax: (202) 544-2260
e-mail: pubs@heritage.org
Web site: www.heritage.org

The Heritage Foundation is a conservative public policy research institute that supports the principles of free enterprise and limited government in environmental matters. Its many publications include the monthly *Policy Review* and position papers concerning terrorism, privacy rights, and constitutional issues.

National Retail Federation (NRF)
325 Seventh St. NW, Suite 1100, Washington, DC   20004
(800) NRF-HOW2 (673-4692) • fax: (202) 737-2849
Web site: www.nrf.com

NRF is a retail trade association with membership that includes retail stores and distributors such as department, discount, catalog, and Internet stores. It aims to expand and improve the retail workforce. The federation opposes privacy legislation that it believes would place too many restrictions on marketers, would burden businesses with too many requirements, or would impede the growth of the Internet. NRF distributes the daily e-mail newsletter *NRF SmartBrief*, the *Weekly Tax Update*, and the monthly *Retail Trade Issues*.

National Security Agency (NSA)

9800 Savage Rd., Fort Meade, MD   20755-6248
(301) 688-6524
Web site: www.nsa.gov

The National Security Agency coordinates, directs, and performs activities which protect American information systems and produce foreign intelligence information. The NSA employs satellites to collect data from telephones and computers, aiding in the fight against terrorism. Speeches, briefings, and reports are available on its Web site.

National Workrights Institute

166 Wall St., Princeton, NJ   08540
(609) 683-0313 • fax: (609) 683-1787
e-mail: info@workrights.org
Web site: www.workrights.org

The National Workrights Institute was founded in January 2000 by the former staff of the American Civil Liberties Union's National Taskforce on Civil Liberties in the Workplace. The institute's goal is to improve the legal protection of human rights in the workplace and to see that employment laws are adequately enforced and strengthened. The institute publishes annual reports and provides information for articles in newspapers, national magazines, and television shows, including *ABC World News Tonight*.

Office of the Privacy Commissioner of Canada

112 Kent St., Place de Ville, Tower B, Third Floor., Ottawa,
   Ontario   K1A 1H3
(800) 282-1376 • fax: (613) 947-6850
e-mail: publications@privcom.gc.ca
Web site: www.privcom.gc.ca

An advocate for the privacy rights of Canadians, the Privacy Commissioner of Canada investigates complaints from individuals with respect to the federal public and the private sectors, conducts audits, and promotes awareness of privacy issues. The Privacy Commissioner's Web site details Canada's privacy legislation, provides privacy impact assessments, and offers various fact sheets. Its Resource Centre contains such publications as the office's annual reports to Parliament, official speeches, and privacy rights guides for businesses and individuals.

Privacy International Washington Office

1718 Connecticut Ave. NW, Suite 200, Washington, DC 20009
(202) 483-1217 • fax: (202) 483-1248
e-mail: privacyint@privacy.org
Web site: www.privacy.org

Privacy International is an independent, nongovernment organization whose goal is to protect the privacy rights of citizens worldwide. On its Web site, the organization provides archives of material on privacy, including international agreements, the report *Freedom of Information and Access to Government Records Around the World,* and *Private Parts Online,* an online newsletter that reports on recent stories on international privacy issues.

Privacy Rights Clearinghouse (PRC)

3100 Fifth Ave., Suite B, San Diego, CA   92103
(619) 298-3396 • fax: (619) 298-5681
e-mail: jbeebe@privacyrights.org
Web site: www.privacyrights.org

The Privacy Rights Clearinghouse (PRC) is a nonprofit consumer organization with a two-part mission—to provide consumer information and advocate for consumer privacy. The group raises awareness of how technology affects personal privacy, empowers consumers to take action to control their own personal information by providing practical tips on privacy protection, responds to privacy-related complaints from consumers, and reports this information. Its Web site provides transcripts of PRC speeches and testimony, stories of consumer experiences, and numerous fact sheets, including "Protecting Financial Privacy."

Bibliography of Books

Paul Abramson, Steven Pinkerton, and Mark Huppin	*Sexual Rights in America.* New York: New York University Press, 2003.
George J. Annas	*The Rights of Patients: The Authoritative ACLU Guide to the Rights of Patients.* Carbondale: Southern Illinois University Press, 2004.
Clay Calvert	*Voyeur Nation: Media, Privacy, and Peering in Modern Culture.* Boulder, CO: Westview Press, 2000.
Nancy Chang	*Silencing Political Dissent: How Post-September 11 Anti-Terrorism Measures Threaten Our Civil Liberties.* New York: Seven Stories Press, 2002.
Jamie Court	*Corporateering: How Corporate Power Steals Your Personal Freedom—And What You Can Do About It.* New York: Jeremy P. Tarcher/Putnam, 2003.
James X. Dempsey and David Cole	*Terrorism and the Constitution: Sacrificing Civil Liberties in the Name of National Security.* Washington, DC: First Amendment Foundation, 2002.
Joseph W. Eaton	*The Privacy Card: A Low Cost Strategy to Combat Terrorism.* Lanham, MD: Rowman & Littlefield, 2003.
Herbert N. Foerstel	*Refuge of a Scoundrel: The Patriot Act in Libraries.* Westport, CT: Libraries Unlimited, 2004.
Simson Garfinkel	*Database Nation: The Death of Privacy in the 21st Century.* Cambridge, MA: O'Reilly, 2000.

Evan Gerstmann	*Same-Sex Marriage and the Constitution*. Los Angeles: Loyola Marymount University, 2003.
Eric J. Gertler	*Prying Eyes: Protect Your Privacy from People Who Sell to You, Snoop on You, and Steal from You*. New York: Random House Reference, 2004.
Richard A. Glenn	*The Right to Privacy: Rights and Liberties Under the Law*. Santa Barbara, CA: ABC-CLIO, 2003.
John Hagel III and Marc Singer	*Net Worth: Shaping Markets When Customers Make the Rules*. Boston: Harvard Business School Press, 1999.
Richard Hunter	*World Without Secrets: Business, Crime, and Privacy in the Age of Ubiquitous Computing*. New York: John Wiley & Sons, 2002.
Bruce Kasanoff	*Making It Personal: How to Profit from Personalization Without Invading Privacy*. Cambridge, MA: Perseus, 2001.
Frederick S. Lane	*The Naked Employee: How Technology Is Compromising Workplace Privacy*. New York: AMACOM Books, 2003.
Al Lautenslager	*Ultimate Guide to Direct Marketing*. Irvine, CA: Entrepreneur Press, 2005.
David Lyon	*Surveillance After September 11*. Cambridge, England: Polity Press, 2003.
Raneta Lawson Mack and Michael J. Kelly	*Equal Justice in the Balance: America's Legal Responses to the Emerging Terrorist Threat*. Ann Arbor: University of Michigan Press, 2004.

Albert J. Marcella and Carol Stucki	*Privacy Handbook: Guidelines, Exposures, Policy Implementation, and International Issues.* Hoboken, NJ: John Wiley & Sons, 2003.
C. William Michaels	*No Greater Threat: America After September 11 and the Rise of a National Security State.* New York: Algora Publishing, 2002.
Mark Monmonier	*Spying with Maps: Surveillance Technologies and the Future of Privacy.* Chicago: University of Chicago Press, 2002.
Donald J. Musch, ed.	*Civil Liberties and the Foreign Intelligence Surveillance Act.* Dobbs Ferry, NY: Oceana Publications, 2003.
Robert O'Harrow Jr.	*No Place to Hide.* New York: Free Press, 2005.
Jeffrey Rosen	*The Naked Crowd: Reclaiming Security and Freedom in an Anxious Age.* New York: Random House, 2004.
Charles J. Sykes	*The End of Privacy: Personal Rights in the Surveillance Society.* New York: St. Martin's Press, 1999.
Reg Whitaker	*The End of Privacy: How Total Surveillance Is Becoming a Reality.* New York: New Press, 1999.

Reports

Robert W. Hahn	*An Assessment of the Costs of Proposed Online Privacy Legislation.* Washington, DC: Association for Competitive Technology, May 7, 2001. www.bbbonline.org.

Philippa Jeffery

Keeping Big Brother from Watching You: Privacy in the Internet Age. Washington, DC: Citizens Against Government Waste, May 14, 2001. www.cgaw.org.

Ed Mierzwinski et al., eds.

The Clean Credit and Identity Theft Protections Act: Model State Laws. Washington, DC: State Public Interest Research Groups and Consumers Union of U.S., Inc., November 2005. www.uspirg.org.

National Forum on Education Statistics

Forum Guide to Protecting the Privacy of Student Information: State and Local Education Agencies. NCES 2004-330. Washington, DC: National Forum on Education Statistics, 2004. www.nces.ed.gov.

Marc Rotenberg and Cedric Laurant

Privacy and Human Rights 2004: An International Survey of Privacy Laws and Developments. Washington, DC: Electronic Privacy Information Center and Privacy International, November 17, 2004. www.privacy.international.org.

U.S. Congress

Tools Against Terror: How the Administration Is Implementing New Laws in the Fight to Protect Our Homeland. Washington, DC: U.S. Government Printing Office, 2004. www.gpoaccess.gov.

Philip Ward

The Identity Cards Bill. Research Paper 05/43. London, England: House of Commons Library, June 13, 2005. www.parliament.uk.

Index